Timed Division Facts
Drills Improve Speed and Accuracy

Grades 4-6

IIIIIIIIIIIIIIIIIIIIIIIIII
I0110608

Written by Ruth Solski
Illustrated by S&S Learning Materials

About the author:

Ruth Solski was an educator for 30 years. Ruth has written many educational resources over the years and is the founder of S&S Learning Materials. As a writer, her main goal is to provide teachers with a useful tool that they can implement in their classrooms to bring the joy of learning to children.

ISBN 978-1-55035-901-5
Copyright 2008
All Rights Reserved * Printed in Canada

Published in the United States by:
On The Mark Press
3909 Witmer Road PMB 175
Niagara Falls, New York
14305
www.onthemarkpress.com

Published in Canada by:
S&S Learning Materials
15 Dairy Avenue
Napanee, Ontario
K7R 1M4
www.sslearning.com

At A Glance

Learning Expectations	Pages 4 to 7	Pages 8 to 11	Pages 12 to 15	Pages 16 to 19	Pages 20 to 21	Pages 22 to 25	Pages 26 to 29	Pages 30 to 33	Pages 34 to 37	Pages 38 to 39	Pages 40 to 46
Division Facts											
• To strengthen division fact recall	•	•	•	•	•	•	•	•	•	•	•
• Improve speed and accuracy in division facts	•	•	•	•	•	•	•	•	•	•	•
• Develop the ability to memorize	•	•	•	•	•	•	•	•	•	•	•
Timed Drills											
• Dividing by two	•										
• Dividing by three		•									
• Dividing by four			•								
• Dividing by five				•							
• Dividing by two to five reviews					•						
• Dividing by six						•					
• Dividing by seven							•				
• Dividing by eight								•			
• Dividing by nine									•		
• Dividing by six to nine reviews										•	
• Reviews of all division facts											•

Timed Division Facts
Drills Improve Speed and Accuracy

Table of Contents

A Note to the Teacher:

The division fact drills have been designed to help strengthen students' speed and accuracy through practice during a specified time or each student could be timed individually.

Some of the drills are shorter and are to be completed on a specified day. Each drill page concentrates on a specific area in division fact recall. The drills proceed from the easiest level to the most difficult level. Each level has a daily practise page, a home practise page, an extra practise page, and a review test page.

The daily practice page is divided into five days. Each day of the week the student is to complete a drill, the date, score, and time it took to do the drill are to be recorded in each section. This page could be glued into the students' work books or kept in individual file folders.

The home practice page is to be sent home to practice fact recall with parent supervision. Once completed, it is to be returned to school signed by a parent. A letter of explanation should be sent home with the first home practice page explaining how it is to be completed.

The extra practice drill sheet is to be used with students who are still having difficulty recalling facts quickly and accurately. It is a different approach to the time drill method. The student must complete the fact with its missing number.

The review page or test page is to be used to test speed and accuracy within a given length of time. Begin with five minutes graduating down to one minute.

Tell students when to begin and when to stop. Have the students circle the last completed question with a red crayon or red pencil crayon. The students are to exchange their papers and to mark each incorrect answer with a red dot as you read the answers aloud. Have the students count the number of correct answers. No credit is to be given for incomplete answers. The student is to record the number of correct answers, time, and date on each sheet where indicated. On each review test have all incomplete answers finished for extra practice after the completed answers have been marked.

There are two timed review tests for each section that may be used after each section has been practiced successfully. These tests will evaluate students' speed and accuracy in each section.

The final drill pages test all the division facts. These pages are to be used in the same manner as the other drills.

The results of the various drills may be recorded on the Score Record Sheets provided in this book.

Dividing by Two Drills

Name: _____

Date: Monday _____   Score: _____ /25   Time: _____ Min. _____ Sec.

2 ÷ 2 = ____	16 ÷ 2 = ____	6 ÷ 2 = ____	4 ÷ 2 = ____	12 ÷ 2 = ____
6 ÷ 2 = ____	4 ÷ 2 = ____	12 ÷ 2 = ____	10 ÷ 2 = ____	18 ÷ 2 = ____
12 ÷ 2 = ____	10 ÷ 2 = ____	18 ÷ 2 = ____	14 ÷ 2 = ____	8 ÷ 2 = ____
18 ÷ 2 = ____	14 ÷ 2 = ____	8 ÷ 2 = ____	2 ÷ 2 = ____	16 ÷ 2 = ____
8 ÷ 2 = ____	2 ÷ 2 = ____	16 ÷ 2 = ____	6 ÷ 2 = ____	4 ÷ 2 = ____

Date: Tuesday _____   Score: _____ /25   Time: _____ Min. _____ Sec.

10 ÷ 2 = ____	18 ÷ 2 = ____	14 ÷ 2 = ____	8 ÷ 2 = ____	2 ÷ 2 = ____
14 ÷ 2 = ____	8 ÷ 2 = ____	2 ÷ 2 = ____	16 ÷ 2 = ____	6 ÷ 2 = ____
2 ÷ 2 = ____	16 ÷ 2 = ____	6 ÷ 2 = ____	4 ÷ 2 = ____	12 ÷ 2 = ____
6 ÷ 2 = ____	4 ÷ 2 = ____	12 ÷ 2 = ____	10 ÷ 2 = ____	18 ÷ 2 = ____
12 ÷ 2 = ____	10 ÷ 2 = ____	18 ÷ 2 = ____	14 ÷ 2 = ____	8 ÷ 2 = ____

Date: Wednesday _____   Score: _____ /25   Time: _____ Min. _____ Sec.

16 ÷ 2 = ____	6 ÷ 2 = ____	4 ÷ 2 = ____	12 ÷ 2 = ____	10 ÷ 2 = ____
4 ÷ 2 = ____	12 ÷ 2 = ____	10 ÷ 2 = ____	18 ÷ 2 = ____	14 ÷ 2 = ____
10 ÷ 2 = ____	18 ÷ 2 = ____	14 ÷ 2 = ____	8 ÷ 2 = ____	2 ÷ 2 = ____
14 ÷ 2 = ____	8 ÷ 2 = ____	2 ÷ 2 = ____	16 ÷ 2 = ____	6 ÷ 2 = ____
2 ÷ 2 = ____	16 ÷ 2 = ____	6 ÷ 2 = ____	4 ÷ 2 = ____	12 ÷ 2 = ____

Date: Thursday _____   Score: _____ /25   Time: _____ Min. _____ Sec.

2 ÷ 2 = ____	16 ÷ 2 = ____	6 ÷ 2 = ____	4 ÷ 2 = ____	12 ÷ 2 = ____
6 ÷ 2 = ____	4 ÷ 2 = ____	12 ÷ 2 = ____	10 ÷ 2 = ____	18 ÷ 2 = ____
12 ÷ 2 = ____	10 ÷ 2 = ____	18 ÷ 2 = ____	14 ÷ 2 = ____	8 ÷ 2 = ____
18 ÷ 2 = ____	14 ÷ 2 = ____	8 ÷ 2 = ____	2 ÷ 2 = ____	16 ÷ 2 = ____
8 ÷ 2 = ____	2 ÷ 2 = ____	16 ÷ 2 = ____	6 ÷ 2 = ____	4 ÷ 2 = ____

Date: Friday _____   Score: _____ /25   Time: _____ Min. _____ Sec.

10 ÷ 2 = ____	18 ÷ 2 = ____	14 ÷ 2 = ____	8 ÷ 2 = ____	2 ÷ 2 = ____
14 ÷ 2 = ____	8 ÷ 2 = ____	2 ÷ 2 = ____	16 ÷ 2 = ____	6 ÷ 2 = ____
2 ÷ 2 = ____	16 ÷ 2 = ____	6 ÷ 2 = ____	4 ÷ 2 = ____	12 ÷ 2 = ____
6 ÷ 2 = ____	4 ÷ 2 = ____	12 ÷ 2 = ____	10 ÷ 2 = ____	18 ÷ 2 = ____
12 ÷ 2 = ____	10 ÷ 2 = ____	18 ÷ 2 = ____	14 ÷ 2 = ____	8 ÷ 2 = ____

Home Practice Dividing by Two Drills

Name: _____

Monday	Tuesday	Wednesday	Thursday	Friday
10 ÷ 2 = ____	16 ÷ 2 = ____	2 ÷ 2 = ____	10 ÷ 2 = ____	2 ÷ 2 = ____
14 ÷ 2 = ____	4 ÷ 2 = ____	6 ÷ 2 = ____	14 ÷ 2 = ____	6 ÷ 2 = ____
2 ÷ 2 = ____	10 ÷ 2 = ____	12 ÷ 2 = ____	2 ÷ 2 = ____	12 ÷ 2 = ____
6 ÷ 2 = ____	14 ÷ 2 = ____	18 ÷ 2 = ____	6 ÷ 2 = ____	18 ÷ 2 = ____
12 ÷ 2 = ____	2 ÷ 2 = ____	8 ÷ 2 = ____	12 ÷ 2 = ____	8 ÷ 2 = ____
18 ÷ 2 = ____	6 ÷ 2 = ____	16 ÷ 2 = ____	18 ÷ 2 = ____	16 ÷ 2 = ____
8 ÷ 2 = ____	12 ÷ 2 = ____	4 ÷ 2 = ____	8 ÷ 2 = ____	4 ÷ 2 = ____
16 ÷ 2 = ____	18 ÷ 2 = ____	10 ÷ 2 = ____	16 ÷ 2 = ____	10 ÷ 2 = ____
4 ÷ 2 = ____	8 ÷ 2 = ____	14 ÷ 2 = ____	4 ÷ 2 = ____	14 ÷ 2 = ____
10 ÷ 2 = ____	16 ÷ 2 = ____	2 ÷ 2 = ____	10 ÷ 2 = ____	2 ÷ 2 = ____
14 ÷ 2 = ____	4 ÷ 2 = ____	6 ÷ 2 = ____	14 ÷ 2 = ____	6 ÷ 2 = ____
2 ÷ 2 = ____	10 ÷ 2 = ____	12 ÷ 2 = ____	2 ÷ 2 = ____	12 ÷ 2 = ____
6 ÷ 2 = ____	14 ÷ 2 = ____	18 ÷ 2 = ____	6 ÷ 2 = ____	18 ÷ 2 = ____
12 ÷ 2 = ____	2 ÷ 2 = ____	8 ÷ 2 = ____	12 ÷ 2 = ____	8 ÷ 2 = ____
18 ÷ 2 = ____	6 ÷ 2 = ____	16 ÷ 2 = ____	18 ÷ 2 = ____	16 ÷ 2 = ____
8 ÷ 2 = ____	12 ÷ 2 = ____	4 ÷ 2 = ____	8 ÷ 2 = ____	4 ÷ 2 = ____
16 ÷ 2 = ____	18 ÷ 2 = ____	10 ÷ 2 = ____	16 ÷ 2 = ____	10 ÷ 2 = ____
4 ÷ 2 = ____	8 ÷ 2 = ____	14 ÷ 2 = ____	4 ÷ 2 = ____	14 ÷ 2 = ____
10 ÷ 2 = ____	16 ÷ 2 = ____	2 ÷ 2 = ____	10 ÷ 2 = ____	2 ÷ 2 = ____
14 ÷ 2 = ____	4 ÷ 2 = ____	6 ÷ 2 = ____	14 ÷ 2 = ____	6 ÷ 2 = ____
2 ÷ 2 = ____	10 ÷ 2 = ____	12 ÷ 2 = ____	2 ÷ 2 = ____	12 ÷ 2 = ____
6 ÷ 2 = ____	14 ÷ 2 = ____	18 ÷ 2 = ____	6 ÷ 2 = ____	18 ÷ 2 = ____
12 ÷ 2 = ____	2 ÷ 2 = ____	8 ÷ 2 = ____	12 ÷ 2 = ____	8 ÷ 2 = ____
18 ÷ 2 = ____	6 ÷ 2 = ____	16 ÷ 2 = ____	18 ÷ 2 = ____	16 ÷ 2 = ____
8 ÷ 2 = ____	12 ÷ 2 = ____	4 ÷ 2 = ____	8 ÷ 2 = ____	4 ÷ 2 = ____
Score: ____/25	Score: ____/25	Score: ____/25	Score: ____/25	Score: ____/25
____ Min.	____ Min.	____ Min.	____ Min.	____ Min.
____ Sec.	____ Sec.	____ Sec.	____ Sec.	____ Sec.

Extra Practice Dividing by Two Drills

Name: _____

Day 1	Day 2	Day 3	Day 4	Day 5
2 ÷ ___ = 0	10 ÷ ___ = 5	___ ÷ 2 = 8	2 ÷ 2 = ___	10 ÷ 2 = ___
___ ÷ 2 = 3	___ ÷ 2 = 7	___ ÷ 2 = 2	6 ÷ 2 = ___	14 ÷ 2 = ___
12 ÷ 2 = ___	2 ÷ 2 = ___	___ ÷ 2 = 5	12 ÷ 2 = ___	2 ÷ 2 = ___
18 ÷ ___ = 9	6 ÷ ___ = 3	___ ÷ 2 = 7	18 ÷ 2 = ___	___ ÷ 2 = 3
___ ÷ 2 = 4	___ ÷ 2 = 6	___ ÷ 2 = 0	8 ÷ 2 = ___	___ ÷ 2 = 6
16 ÷ 2 = ___	18 ÷ 2 = ___	___ ÷ 2 = 3	16 ÷ 2 = ___	___ ÷ 2 = 9
4 ÷ ___ = 2	8 ÷ ___ = 4	___ ÷ 2 = 6	4 ÷ 2 = ___	___ ÷ 2 = 4
___ ÷ 2 = 5	___ ÷ 2 = 8	___ ÷ 2 = 9	10 ÷ 2 = ___	___ ÷ 2 = 8
14 ÷ 2 = ___	4 ÷ 2 = ___	___ ÷ 2 = 4	14 ÷ 2 = ___	___ ÷ 2 = 2
2 ÷ ___ = 0	14 ÷ ___ = 7	___ ÷ 2 = 8	2 ÷ 2 = ___	18 ÷ 2 = ___
___ ÷ 2 = 6	___ ÷ 2 = 5	___ ÷ 2 = 2	6 ÷ 2 = ___	16 ÷ 2 = ___
6 ÷ 2 = ___	2 ÷ 2 = ___	___ ÷ 2 = 5	12 ÷ 2 = ___	12 ÷ 2 = ___
18 ÷ ___ = 9	6 ÷ ___ = 3	___ ÷ 2 = 7	18 ÷ 2 = ___	___ ÷ 2 = 0
___ ÷ 2 = 4	___ ÷ 2 = 6	___ ÷ 2 = 0	8 ÷ 2 = ___	___ ÷ 2 = 3
4 ÷ 2 = ___	18 ÷ 2 = ___	___ ÷ 2 = 3	16 ÷ 2 = ___	___ ÷ 2 = 6
16 ÷ ___ = 8	16 ÷ ___ = 8	___ ÷ 2 = 6	4 ÷ 2 = ___	___ ÷ 2 = 9
___ ÷ 2 = 2	___ ÷ 2 = 4	___ ÷ 2 = 9	10 ÷ 2 = ___	___ ÷ 2 = 4
10 ÷ 2 = ___	4 ÷ 2 = ___	___ ÷ 2 = 4	14 ÷ 2 = ___	___ ÷ 2 = 8
___ ÷ 2 = 0	10 ÷ ___ = 5	___ ÷ 2 = 8	2 ÷ 2 = ___	4 ÷ 2 = ___
14 ÷ ___ = 7	___ ÷ 2 = 7	___ ÷ 2 = 4	6 ÷ 2 = ___	10 ÷ 2 = ___
6 ÷ 2 = ___	16 ÷ 2 = ___	___ ÷ 2 = 5	12 ÷ 2 = ___	14 ÷ 2 = ___
___ ÷ 2 = 9	2 ÷ ___ = 0	___ ÷ 2 = 7	18 ÷ 2 = ___	___ ÷ 2 = 0
12 ÷ ___ = 6	___ ÷ 2 = 3	___ ÷ 2 = 0	8 ÷ 2 = ___	___ ÷ 2 = 6
8 ÷ 2 = ___	12 ÷ 2 = ___	___ ÷ 2 = 3	16 ÷ 2 = ___	___ ÷ 2 = 9
___ ÷ 2 = 8	18 ÷ ___ = 9	___ ÷ 2 = 6	4 ÷ 2 = ___	___ ÷ 2 = 8
Score: _____ /25	Score: _____ /25	Score: _____ /25	Score: _____ /25	Score: _____ /25
_____ Min.	_____ Min.	_____ Min.	_____ Min.	_____ Min.
_____ Sec.	_____ Sec.	_____ Sec.	_____ Sec.	_____ Sec.

OTM-1142 • SSK1-42 Timed Division Facts

Dividing by Two Review Test

Name: _____

A									
$2\overline{)6}$	$2\overline{)10}$	$2\overline{)8}$	$2\overline{)2}$	$2\overline{)16}$	$2\overline{)4}$	$2\overline{)10}$	$2\overline{)12}$	$2\overline{)14}$	$2\overline{)18}$

B									
$2\overline{)10}$	$2\overline{)8}$	$2\overline{)12}$	$2\overline{)18}$	$2\overline{)14}$	$2\overline{)6}$	$2\overline{)8}$	$2\overline{)16}$	$2\overline{)18}$	$2\overline{)2}$

C									
$2\overline{)12}$	$2\overline{)4}$	$2\overline{)2}$	$2\overline{)8}$	$2\overline{)10}$	$2\overline{)14}$	$2\overline{)18}$	$2\overline{)6}$	$2\overline{)16}$	$2\overline{)12}$

D									
$2\overline{)4}$	$2\overline{)12}$	$2\overline{)8}$	$2\overline{)14}$	$2\overline{)4}$	$2\overline{)18}$	$2\overline{)10}$	$2\overline{)6}$	$2\overline{)16}$	$2\overline{)10}$

E									
$2\overline{)4}$	$2\overline{)8}$	$2\overline{)6}$	$2\overline{)14}$	$2\overline{)16}$	$2\overline{)10}$	$2\overline{)18}$	$2\overline{)2}$	$2\overline{)12}$	$2\overline{)2}$

F									
$2\overline{)6}$	$2\overline{)10}$	$2\overline{)4}$	$2\overline{)12}$	$2\overline{)2}$	$2\overline{)14}$	$2\overline{)16}$	$2\overline{)18}$	$2\overline{)4}$	$2\overline{)8}$

G									
$2\overline{)10}$	$2\overline{)6}$	$2\overline{)14}$	$2\overline{)18}$	$2\overline{)2}$	$2\overline{)8}$	$2\overline{)12}$	$2\overline{)16}$	$2\overline{)2}$	$2\overline{)4}$

H									
$2\overline{)6}$	$2\overline{)4}$	$2\overline{)14}$	$2\overline{)2}$	$2\overline{)12}$	$2\overline{)18}$	$2\overline{)16}$	$2\overline{)10}$	$2\overline{)8}$	$2\overline{)10}$

I									
$2\overline{)4}$	$2\overline{)8}$	$2\overline{)16}$	$2\overline{)14}$	$2\overline{)6}$	$2\overline{)12}$	$2\overline{)16}$	$2\overline{)18}$	$2\overline{)10}$	$2\overline{)2}$

J									
$2\overline{)16}$	$2\overline{)2}$	$2\overline{)18}$	$2\overline{)4}$	$2\overline{)14}$	$2\overline{)16}$	$2\overline{)12}$	$2\overline{)10}$	$2\overline{)6}$	$2\overline{)8}$

Date: _____   Score: _____/100   Time: _____ Min. _____ Sec.

Dividing by Three Drills

Name: _____

Date: Monday _____ Score: _____ /25 Time: _____ Min. _____ Sec.

$3 \div 3 =$ ___	$27 \div 3 =$ ___	$18 \div 3 =$ ___	$15 \div 3 =$ ___	$6 \div 3 =$ ___
$18 \div 3 =$ ___	$15 \div 3 =$ ___	$6 \div 3 =$ ___	$9 \div 3 =$ ___	$24 \div 3 =$ ___
$6 \div 3 =$ ___	$9 \div 3 =$ ___	$24 \div 3 =$ ___	$21 \div 3 =$ ___	$12 \div 3 =$ ___
$24 \div 3 =$ ___	$21 \div 3 =$ ___	$12 \div 3 =$ ___	$3 \div 3 =$ ___	$27 \div 3 =$ ___
$12 \div 3 =$ ___	$3 \div 3 =$ ___	$27 \div 3 =$ ___	$18 \div 3 =$ ___	$15 \div 3 =$ ___

Date: Tuesday _____ Score: _____ /25 Time: _____ Min. _____ Sec.

$9 \div 3 =$ ___	$24 \div 3 =$ ___	$21 \div 3 =$ ___	$12 \div 3 =$ ___	$3 \div 3 =$ ___
$21 \div 3 =$ ___	$12 \div 3 =$ ___	$3 \div 3 =$ ___	$27 \div 3 =$ ___	$18 \div 3 =$ ___
$3 \div 3 =$ ___	$27 \div 3 =$ ___	$18 \div 3 =$ ___	$15 \div 3 =$ ___	$6 \div 3 =$ ___
$18 \div 3 =$ ___	$15 \div 3 =$ ___	$6 \div 3 =$ ___	$9 \div 3 =$ ___	$24 \div 3 =$ ___
$6 \div 3 =$ ___	$9 \div 3 =$ ___	$24 \div 3 =$ ___	$21 \div 3 =$ ___	$12 \div 3 =$ ___

Date: Wednesday _____ Score: _____ /25 Time: _____ Min. _____ Sec.

$27 \div 3 =$ ___	$18 \div 3 =$ ___	$15 \div 3 =$ ___	$6 \div 3 =$ ___	$9 \div 3 =$ ___
$15 \div 3 =$ ___	$6 \div 3 =$ ___	$9 \div 3 =$ ___	$24 \div 3 =$ ___	$21 \div 3 =$ ___
$9 \div 3 =$ ___	$24 \div 3 =$ ___	$21 \div 3 =$ ___	$12 \div 3 =$ ___	$3 \div 3 =$ ___
$21 \div 3 =$ ___	$12 \div 3 =$ ___	$3 \div 3 =$ ___	$27 \div 3 =$ ___	$18 \div 3 =$ ___
$3 \div 3 =$ ___	$27 \div 3 =$ ___	$18 \div 3 =$ ___	$15 \div 3 =$ ___	$6 \div 3 =$ ___

Date: Thursday _____ Score: _____ /25 Time: _____ Min. _____ Sec.

$24 \div 3 =$ ___	$21 \div 3 =$ ___	$12 \div 3 =$ ___	$3 \div 3 =$ ___	$27 \div 3 =$ ___
$12 \div 3 =$ ___	$3 \div 3 =$ ___	$27 \div 3 =$ ___	$18 \div 3 =$ ___	$15 \div 3 =$ ___
$27 \div 3 =$ ___	$18 \div 3 =$ ___	$15 \div 3 =$ ___	$6 \div 3 =$ ___	$9 \div 3 =$ ___
$15 \div 3 =$ ___	$6 \div 3 =$ ___	$9 \div 3 =$ ___	$24 \div 3 =$ ___	$21 \div 3 =$ ___
$9 \div 3 =$ ___	$24 \div 3 =$ ___	$21 \div 3 =$ ___	$12 \div 3 =$ ___	$3 \div 3 =$ ___

Date: Friday _____ Score: _____ /25 Time: _____ Min. _____ Sec.

$18 \div 3 =$ ___	$15 \div 3 =$ ___	$6 \div 3 =$ ___	$9 \div 3 =$ ___	$24 \div 3 =$ ___
$6 \div 3 =$ ___	$9 \div 3 =$ ___	$24 \div 3 =$ ___	$21 \div 3 =$ ___	$12 \div 3 =$ ___
$24 \div 3 =$ ___	$21 \div 3 =$ ___	$12 \div 3 =$ ___	$3 \div 3 =$ ___	$27 \div 3 =$ ___
$12 \div 3 =$ ___	$3 \div 3 =$ ___	$27 \div 3 =$ ___	$18 \div 3 =$ ___	$15 \div 3 =$ ___
$27 \div 3 =$ ___	$18 \div 3 =$ ___	$15 \div 3 =$ ___	$6 \div 3 =$ ___	$9 \div 3 =$ ___

Home Practice Dividing by Three Drills

Name: _____

Monday	Tuesday	Wednesday	Thursday	Friday
3 ÷ 3 = ____	9 ÷ 3 = ____	27 ÷ 3 = ____	24 ÷ 3 = ____	18 ÷ 3 = ____
18 ÷ 3 = ____	21 ÷ 3 = ____	15 ÷ 3 = ____	12 ÷ 3 = ____	6 ÷ 3 = ____
6 ÷ 3 = ____	3 ÷ 3 = ____	9 ÷ 3 = ____	27 ÷ 3 = ____	24 ÷ 3 = ____
24 ÷ 3 = ____	18 ÷ 3 = ____	21 ÷ 3 = ____	15 ÷ 3 = ____	12 ÷ 3 = ____
12 ÷ 3 = ____	6 ÷ 3 = ____	3 ÷ 3 = ____	9 ÷ 3 = ____	27 ÷ 3 = ____
27 ÷ 3 = ____	24 ÷ 3 = ____	18 ÷ 3 = ____	21 ÷ 3 = ____	15 ÷ 3 = ____
15 ÷ 3 = ____	12 ÷ 3 = ____	6 ÷ 3 = ____	3 ÷ 3 = ____	9 ÷ 3 = ____
9 ÷ 3 = ____	27 ÷ 3 = ____	24 ÷ 3 = ____	18 ÷ 3 = ____	21 ÷ 3 = ____
21 ÷ 3 = ____	15 ÷ 3 = ____	12 ÷ 3 = ____	6 ÷ 3 = ____	3 ÷ 3 = ____
3 ÷ 3 = ____	9 ÷ 3 = ____	27 ÷ 3 = ____	24 ÷ 3 = ____	18 ÷ 3 = ____
18 ÷ 3 = ____	21 ÷ 3 = ____	15 ÷ 3 = ____	12 ÷ 3 = ____	6 ÷ 3 = ____
6 ÷ 3 = ____	3 ÷ 3 = ____	9 ÷ 3 = ____	27 ÷ 3 = ____	24 ÷ 3 = ____
24 ÷ 3 = ____	18 ÷ 3 = ____	21 ÷ 3 = ____	15 ÷ 3 = ____	12 ÷ 3 = ____
12 ÷ 3 = ____	6 ÷ 3 = ____	3 ÷ 3 = ____	9 ÷ 3 = ____	27 ÷ 3 = ____
27 ÷ 3 = ____	24 ÷ 3 = ____	18 ÷ 3 = ____	21 ÷ 3 = ____	15 ÷ 3 = ____
15 ÷ 3 = ____	12 ÷ 3 = ____	6 ÷ 3 = ____	3 ÷ 3 = ____	9 ÷ 3 = ____
9 ÷ 3 = ____	27 ÷ 3 = ____	24 ÷ 3 = ____	18 ÷ 3 = ____	21 ÷ 3 = ____
21 ÷ 3 = ____	15 ÷ 3 = ____	12 ÷ 3 = ____	6 ÷ 3 = ____	3 ÷ 3 = ____
3 ÷ 3 = ____	9 ÷ 3 = ____	27 ÷ 3 = ____	24 ÷ 3 = ____	18 ÷ 3 = ____
18 ÷ 3 = ____	21 ÷ 3 = ____	15 ÷ 3 = ____	12 ÷ 3 = ____	6 ÷ 3 = ____
6 ÷ 3 = ____	3 ÷ 3 = ____	9 ÷ 3 = ____	27 ÷ 3 = ____	24 ÷ 3 = ____
24 ÷ 3 = ____	18 ÷ 3 = ____	21 ÷ 3 = ____	15 ÷ 3 = ____	12 ÷ 3 = ____
12 ÷ 3 = ____	6 ÷ 3 = ____	3 ÷ 3 = ____	9 ÷ 3 = ____	27 ÷ 3 = ____
27 ÷ 3 = ____	24 ÷ 3 = ____	18 ÷ 3 = ____	21 ÷ 3 = ____	15 ÷ 3 = ____
15 ÷ 3 = ____	12 ÷ 3 = ____	6 ÷ 3 = ____	3 ÷ 3 = ____	9 ÷ 3 = ____
Score: ____/25 _____ Min. _____ Sec.	Score: ____/25 _____ Min. _____ Sec.	Score: ____/25 _____ Min. _____ Sec.	Score: ____/25 _____ Min. _____ Sec.	Score: ____/25 _____ Min. _____ Sec.

Extra Practice Dividing by Three Drills

Name: _____

Day 1	Day 2	Day 3	Day 4	Day 5
$3 \div \underline{\quad} = 1$	$24 \div \underline{\quad} = 8$	$\underline{\quad} \div 3 = 3$	$6 \div 3 = \underline{\quad}$	$3 \div 3 = \underline{\quad}$
$\underline{\quad} \div 3 = 6$	$\underline{\quad} \div 3 = 4$	$\underline{\quad} \div 3 = 5$	$21 \div 3 = \underline{\quad}$	$18 \div 3 = \underline{\quad}$
$27 \div 3 = \underline{\quad}$	$3 \div 3 = \underline{\quad}$	$\underline{\quad} \div 3 = 8$	$9 \div 3 = \underline{\quad}$	$27 \div 3 = \underline{\quad}$
$6 \div \underline{\quad} = 2$	$18 \div \underline{\quad} = 6$	$\underline{\quad} \div 3 = 4$	$15 \div 3 = \underline{\quad}$	$\underline{\quad} \div 3 = 2$
$\underline{\quad} \div 3 = 7$	$\underline{\quad} \div 3 = 9$	$\underline{\quad} \div 3 = 1$	$24 \div 3 = \underline{\quad}$	$\underline{\quad} \div 3 = 7$
$9 \div 3 = \underline{\quad}$	$6 \div 3 = \underline{\quad}$	$\underline{\quad} \div 3 = 6$	$12 \div 3 = \underline{\quad}$	$\underline{\quad} \div 3 = 3$
$15 \div \underline{\quad} = 5$	$21 \div \underline{\quad} = 7$	$\underline{\quad} \div 3 = 9$	$3 \div 3 = \underline{\quad}$	$\underline{\quad} \div 3 = 5$
$\underline{\quad} \div 3 = 8$	$\underline{\quad} \div 3 = 3$	$\underline{\quad} \div 3 = 2$	$18 \div 3 = \underline{\quad}$	$\underline{\quad} \div 3 = 8$
$12 \div 3 = \underline{\quad}$	$15 \div 3 = \underline{\quad}$	$\underline{\quad} \div 3 = 7$	$27 \div 3 = \underline{\quad}$	$\underline{\quad} \div 3 = 4$
$3 \div \underline{\quad} = 1$	$12 \div \underline{\quad} = 4$	$\underline{\quad} \div 3 = 3$	$6 \div 3 = \underline{\quad}$	$3 \div 3 = \underline{\quad}$
$\underline{\quad} \div 3 = 6$	$\underline{\quad} \div 3 = 8$	$\underline{\quad} \div 3 = 5$	$21 \div 3 = \underline{\quad}$	$18 \div 3 = \underline{\quad}$
$6 \div 3 = \underline{\quad}$	$3 \div 3 = \underline{\quad}$	$\underline{\quad} \div 3 = 8$	$9 \div 3 = \underline{\quad}$	$6 \div 3 = \underline{\quad}$
$27 \div \underline{\quad} = 9$	$18 \div \underline{\quad} = 6$	$\underline{\quad} \div 3 = 4$	$15 \div 3 = \underline{\quad}$	$\underline{\quad} \div 3 = 9$
$\underline{\quad} \div 3 = 7$	$\underline{\quad} \div 3 = 9$	$\underline{\quad} \div 3 = 1$	$24 \div 3 = \underline{\quad}$	$\underline{\quad} \div 3 = 2$
$9 \div 3 = \underline{\quad}$	$21 \div 3 = \underline{\quad}$	$\underline{\quad} \div 3 = 6$	$12 \div 3 = \underline{\quad}$	$\underline{\quad} \div 3 = 7$
$24 \div \underline{\quad} = 8$	$6 \div \underline{\quad} = 2$	$\underline{\quad} \div 3 = 9$	$3 \div 3 = \underline{\quad}$	$\underline{\quad} \div 3 = 3$
$\underline{\quad} \div 3 = 5$	$\underline{\quad} \div 3 = 3$	$\underline{\quad} \div 3 = 2$	$18 \div 3 = \underline{\quad}$	$\underline{\quad} \div 3 = 5$
$12 \div 3 = \underline{\quad}$	$15 \div 3 = \underline{\quad}$	$\underline{\quad} \div 3 = 7$	$27 \div 3 = \underline{\quad}$	$\underline{\quad} \div 3 = 8$
$3 \div \underline{\quad} = 1$	$24 \div \underline{\quad} = 8$	$\underline{\quad} \div 3 = 3$	$6 \div 3 = \underline{\quad}$	$12 \div 3 = \underline{\quad}$
$\underline{\quad} \div 3 = 6$	$\underline{\quad} \div 3 = 4$	$\underline{\quad} \div 3 = 5$	$21 \div 3 = \underline{\quad}$	$18 \div 3 = \underline{\quad}$
$27 \div 3 = \underline{\quad}$	$3 \div 3 = \underline{\quad}$	$\underline{\quad} \div 3 = 8$	$9 \div 3 = \underline{\quad}$	$27 \div 3 = \underline{\quad}$
$6 \div \underline{\quad} = 2$	$18 \div 3 = \underline{\quad}$	$\underline{\quad} \div 3 = 4$	$15 \div 3 = \underline{\quad}$	$\underline{\quad} \div 3 = 1$
$\underline{\quad} \div 3 = 7$	$\underline{\quad} \div 3 = 9$	$\underline{\quad} \div 3 = 1$	$24 \div 3 = \underline{\quad}$	$\underline{\quad} \div 3 = 6$
$9 \div 3 = \underline{\quad}$	$21 \div 3 = \underline{\quad}$	$\underline{\quad} \div 3 = 6$	$12 \div 3 = \underline{\quad}$	$\underline{\quad} \div 3 = 9$
$15 \div \underline{\quad} = 5$	$6 \div \underline{\quad} = 2$	$\underline{\quad} \div 3 = 9$	$3 \div 3 = \underline{\quad}$	$\underline{\quad} \div 3 = 2$
Score: _____ /25	Score: _____ /25	Score: _____ /25	Score: _____ /25	Score: _____ /25
_____ Min.	_____ Min.	_____ Min.	_____ Min.	_____ Min.
_____ Sec.	_____ Sec.	_____ Sec.	_____ Sec.	_____ Sec.

© On The Mark Press • S&S Learning Materials
OTM-1142 • SSK1-42 Timed Division Facts

Dividing by Three Review Test

Name: _____

A									
3)9	3)27	3)15	3)3	3)24	3)21	3)18	3)12	3)15	3)9

B									
3)12	3)18	3)9	3)27	3)15	3)21	3)3	3)15	3)18	3)6

C									
3)6	3)15	3)21	3)9	3)18	3)12	3)24	3)3	3)27	3)12

D									
3)15	3)27	3)24	3)21	3)18	3)15	3)12	3)9	3)6	3)3

E									
3)6	3)24	3)18	3)9	3)3	3)21	3)18	3)27	3)12	3)15

F									
3)3	3)6	3)9	3)12	3)15	3)18	3)21	3)24	3)27	3)12

G									
3)12	3)24	3)6	3)18	3)3	3)27	3)21	3)9	3)12	3)15

H									
3)15	3)18	3)21	3)3	3)24	3)6	3)27	3)9	3)3	3)12

I									
3)9	3)27	3)12	3)24	3)15	3)21	3)3	3)18	3)6	3)16

J									
3)15	3)21	3)24	3)27	3)18	3)9	3)12	3)9	3)6	3)3

Date: _____   Score: _____ /100   Time: _____ Min. _____ Sec.

OTM-1142 • SSK1-42 Timed Division Facts

Dividing by Four Drills

Name: _____

Date: Monday _____ Score: _____ /25 Time: _____ Min. _____ Sec.

$4 \div 4 =$ ____	$12 \div 4 =$ ____	$20 \div 4 =$ ____	$28 \div 4 =$ ____	$36 \div 4 =$ ____
$20 \div 4 =$ ____	$28 \div 4 =$ ____	$36 \div 4 =$ ____	$16 \div 4 =$ ____	$8 \div 4 =$ ____
$36 \div 4 =$ ____	$16 \div 4 =$ ____	$8 \div 4 =$ ____	$32 \div 4 =$ ____	$24 \div 4 =$ ____
$8 \div 4 =$ ____	$32 \div 4 =$ ____	$24 \div 4 =$ ____	$4 \div 4 =$ ____	$12 \div 4 =$ ____
$24 \div 4 =$ ____	$4 \div 4 =$ ____	$12 \div 4 =$ ____	$20 \div 4 =$ ____	$28 \div 4 =$ ____

Date: Tuesday _____ Score: _____ /25 Time: _____ Min. _____ Sec.

$16 \div 4 =$ ____	$8 \div 4 =$ ____	$32 \div 4 =$ ____	$24 \div 4 =$ ____	$4 \div 4 =$ ____
$32 \div 4 =$ ____	$24 \div 4 =$ ____	$4 \div 4 =$ ____	$12 \div 4 =$ ____	$20 \div 4 =$ ____
$4 \div 4 =$ ____	$12 \div 4 =$ ____	$20 \div 4 =$ ____	$28 \div 4 =$ ____	$36 \div 4 =$ ____
$20 \div 4 =$ ____	$28 \div 4 =$ ____	$36 \div 4 =$ ____	$16 \div 4 =$ ____	$8 \div 4 =$ ____
$36 \div 4 =$ ____	$16 \div 4 =$ ____	$8 \div 4 =$ ____	$32 \div 4 =$ ____	$24 \div 4 =$ ____

Date: Wednesday _____ Score: _____ /25 Time: _____ Min. _____ Sec.

$12 \div 4 =$ ____	$20 \div 4 =$ ____	$28 \div 4 =$ ____	$36 \div 4 =$ ____	$16 \div 4 =$ ____
$28 \div 4 =$ ____	$36 \div 4 =$ ____	$16 \div 4 =$ ____	$8 \div 4 =$ ____	$32 \div 4 =$ ____
$16 \div 4 =$ ____	$8 \div 4 =$ ____	$32 \div 4 =$ ____	$24 \div 4 =$ ____	$4 \div 4 =$ ____
$32 \div 4 =$ ____	$24 \div 4 =$ ____	$4 \div 4 =$ ____	$12 \div 4 =$ ____	$12 \div 4 =$ ____
$4 \div 4 =$ ____	$12 \div 4 =$ ____	$20 \div 4 =$ ____	$28 \div 4 =$ ____	$36 \div 4 =$ ____

Date: Thursday _____ Score: _____ /25 Time: _____ Min. _____ Sec.

$8 \div 4 =$ ____	$32 \div 4 =$ ____	$24 \div 4 =$ ____	$4 \div 4 =$ ____	$12 \div 4 =$ ____
$24 \div 4 =$ ____	$4 \div 4 =$ ____	$12 \div 4 =$ ____	$20 \div ?4 =$ ____	$28 \div 4 =$ ____
$12 \div 4 =$ ____	$20 \div 4 =$ ____	$28 \div 4 =$ ____	$36 \div 4 =$ ____	$16 \div 4 =$ ____
$28 \div 4 =$ ____	$36 \div 4 =$ ____	$16 \div 4 =$ ____	$8 \div 4 =$ ____	$32 \div 4 =$ ____
$16 \div 4 =$ ____	$8 \div 4 =$ ____	$32 \div 4 =$ ____	$24 \div 4 =$ ____	$4 \div 4 =$ ____

Date: Friday _____ Score: _____ /25 Time: _____ Min. _____ Sec.

$20 \div 4 =$ ____	$28 \div 4 =$ ____	$36 \div 4 =$ ____	$16 \div 4 =$ ____	$8 \div 4 =$ ____
$36 \div 4 =$ ____	$16 \div 4 =$ ____	$8 \div 4 =$ ____	$32 \div 4 =$ ____	$24 \div 4 =$ ____
$8 \div 4 =$ ____	$32 \div 4 =$ ____	$24 \div 4 =$ ____	$4 \div 4 =$ ____	$12 \div 4 =$ ____
$24 \div 4 =$ ____	$4 \div 4 =$ ____	$12 \div 4 =$ ____	$20 \div 4 =$ ____	$28 \div 4 =$ ____
$12 \div 4 =$ ____	$20 \div 4 =$ ____	$28 \div 4 =$ ____	$36 \div 4 =$ ____	$16 \div 4 =$ ____

Home Practice Dividing by Four Drills

Name: _____

Monday	Tuesday	Wednesday	Thursday	Friday
16 ÷ 4 = ____	4 ÷ 4 = ____	8 ÷ 4 = ____	12 ÷ 4 = ____	20 ÷ 4 = ____
32 ÷ 4 = ____	20 ÷ 4 = ____	24 ÷ 4 = ____	28 ÷ 4 = ____	36 ÷ 4 = ____
4 ÷ 4 = ____	36 ÷ 4 = ____	12 ÷ 4 = ____	16 ÷ 4 = ____	8 ÷ 4 = ____
20 ÷ 4 = ____	8 ÷ 4 = ____	28 ÷ 4 = ____	32 ÷ 4 = ____	24 ÷ 4 = ____
36 ÷ 4 = ____	24 ÷ 4 = ____	16 ÷ 4 = ____	4 ÷ 4 = ____	12 ÷ 4 = ____
8 ÷ 4 = ____	12 ÷ 4 = ____	32 ÷ 4 = ____	20 ÷ 4 = ____	28 ÷ 4 = ____
24 ÷ 4 = ____	28 ÷ 4 = ____	4 ÷ 4 = ____	36 ÷ 4 = ____	16 ÷ 4 = ____
12 ÷ 4 = ____	16 ÷ 4 = ____	20 ÷ 4 = ____	8 ÷ 4 = ____	32 ÷ 4 = ____
28 ÷ 4 = ____	32 ÷ 4 = ____	36 ÷ 4 = ____	24 ÷ 4 = ____	4 ÷ 4 = ____
16 ÷ 4 = ____	4 ÷ 4 = ____	8 ÷ 4 = ____	12 ÷ 4 = ____	20 ÷ 4 = ____
32 ÷ 4 = ____	20 ÷ 4 = ____	24 ÷ 4 = ____	28 ÷ 4 = ____	36 ÷ 4 = ____
4 ÷ 4 = ____	36 ÷ 4 = ____	12 ÷ 4 = ____	16 ÷ 4 = ____	8 ÷ 4 = ____
20 ÷ 4 = ____	8 ÷ 4 = ____	28 ÷ 4 = ____	32 ÷ 4 = ____	24 ÷ 4 = ____
36 ÷ 4 = ____	24 ÷ 4 = ____	16 ÷ 4 = ____	4 ÷ 4 = ____	12 ÷ 4 = ____
8 ÷ 4 = ____	12 ÷ 4 = ____	32 ÷ 4 = ____	20 ÷ 4 = ____	28 ÷ 4 = ____
24 ÷ 4 = ____	28 ÷ 4 = ____	4 ÷ 4 = ____	36 ÷ 4 = ____	16 ÷ 4 = ____
12 ÷ 4 = ____	16 ÷ 4 = ____	20 ÷ 4 = ____	8 ÷ 4 = ____	32 ÷ 4 = ____
28 ÷ 4 = ____	32 ÷ 4 = ____	36 ÷ 4 = ____	24 ÷ 4 = ____	4 ÷ 4 = ____
16 ÷ 4 = ____	4 ÷ 4 = ____	8 ÷ 4 = ____	12 ÷ 4 = ____	20 ÷ 4 = ____
32 ÷ 4 = ____	20 ÷ 4 = ____	24 ÷ 4 = ____	28 ÷ 4 = ____	36 ÷ 4 = ____
4 ÷ 4 = ____	36 ÷ 4 = ____	12 ÷ 4 = ____	16 ÷ 4 = ____	8 ÷ 4 = ____
20 ÷ 4 = ____	8 ÷ 4 = ____	28 ÷ 4 = ____	32 ÷ 4 = ____	24 ÷ 4 = ____
36 ÷ 4 = ____	24 ÷ 4 = ____	16 ÷ 4 = ____	4 ÷ 4 = ____	12 ÷ 4 = ____
8 ÷ 4 = ____	12 ÷ 4 = ____	32 ÷ 4 = ____	20 ÷ 4 = ____	28 ÷ 4 = ____
24 ÷ 4 = ____	28 ÷ 4 = ____	4 ÷ 4 = ____	36 ÷ 4 = ____	16 ÷ 4 = ____
Score: ____/25 ____ Min. ____ Sec.	Score: ____/25 ____ Min. ____ Sec.	Score: ____/25 ____ Min. ____ Sec.	Score: ____/25 ____ Min. ____ Sec.	Score: ____/25 ____ Min. ____ Sec.

Extra Practice Dividing by Four Drills

Name: _____

Day 1	Day 2	Day 3	Day 4	Day 5
4 ÷ ___ = 1	28 ÷ ___ = 7	___ ÷ 4 = 6	36 ÷ 4 = ___	4 ÷ 4 = ___
___ ÷ 4 = 8	___ ÷ 4 = 5	___ ÷ 4 = 4	12 ÷ 4 = ___	32 ÷ 4 = ___
8 ÷ 4 = ___	4 ÷ 4 = ___	___ ÷ 4 = 7	24 ÷ 4 = ___	8 ÷ 4 = ___
36 ÷ ___ = 9	32 ÷ ___ = 8	___ ÷ 4 = 5	16 ÷ 4 = ___	___ ÷ 4 = 9
___ ÷ 4 = 3	___ ÷ 4 = 2	___ ÷ 4 = 1	28 ÷ 4 = ___	___ ÷ 4 = 3
24 ÷ 4 = ___	36 ÷ 4 = ___	___ ÷ 4 = 8	20 ÷ 4 = ___	___ ÷ 4 = 6
16 ÷ ___ = 4	12 ÷ ___ = 3	___ ÷ 4 = 2	4 ÷ 4 = ___	___ ÷ 4 = 4
___ ÷ 4 = 7	___ ÷ 4 = 6	___ ÷ 4 = 9	32 ÷ 4 = ___	___ ÷ 4 = 7
20 ÷ 4 = ___	16 ÷ 4 = ___	___ ÷ 4 = 3	8 ÷ 4 = ___	___ ÷ 4 = 5
4 ÷ ___ = 1	20 ÷ ___ = 5	___ ÷ 4 = 8	36 ÷ 4 = ___	4 ÷ 4 = ___
___ ÷ 4 = 2	___ ÷ 4 = 7	___ ÷ 4 = 4	12 ÷ 4 = ___	32 ÷ 4 = ___
32 ÷ 4 = ___	32 ÷ 4 = ___	___ ÷ 4 = 7	24 ÷ 4 = ___	8 ÷ 4 = ___
36 ÷ ___ = 9	4 ÷ ___ = 1	___ ÷ 4 = 5	16 ÷ 4 = ___	___ ÷ 4 = 9
___ ÷ 4 = 3	___ ÷ 4 = 2	___ ÷ 4 = 1	28 ÷ 4 = ___	___ ÷ 4 = 3
16 ÷ 4 = ___	36 ÷ 4 = ___	___ ÷ 4 = 8	20 ÷ 4 = ___	___ ÷ 4 = 6
28 ÷ ___ = 7	12 ÷ ___ = 3	___ ÷ 4 = 2	4 ÷ 4 = ___	___ ÷ 4 = 4
___ ÷ 4 = 5	___ ÷ 4 = 6	___ ÷ 4 = 9	32 ÷ 4 = ___	___ ÷ 4 = 5
4 ÷ 4 = ___	16 ÷ 4 = ___	___ ÷ 4 = 3	8 ÷ 4 = ___	___ ÷ 4 = 7
32 ÷ ___ = 8	28 ÷ ___ = 7	___ ÷ 4 = 6	36 ÷ 4 = ___	36 ÷ 4 = ___
___ ÷ 4 = 2	___ ÷ 4 = 5	___ ÷ 4 = 4	12 ÷ 4 = ___	12 ÷ 4 = ___
36 ÷ 4 = ___	4 ÷ 4 = ___	___ ÷ 4 = 7	24 ÷ 4 = ___	24 ÷ 4 = ___
12 ÷ ___ = 3	32 ÷ ___ = 8	___ ÷ 4 = 5	16 ÷ 4 = ___	___ ÷ 4 = 4
___ ÷ 4 = 6	___ ÷ 4 = 2	___ ÷ 4 = 1	28 ÷ 4 = ___	___ ÷ 4 = 6
16 ÷ 4 = ___	36 ÷ 4 = ___	___ ÷ 4 = 8	20 ÷ 4 = ___	___ ÷ 4 = 3
36 ÷ 4 = ___	12 ÷ ___ = 3	___ ÷ 4 = 2	4 ÷ 4 = ___	___ ÷ 4 = 9
Score: ___/25	Score: ___/25	Score: ___/25	Score: ___/25	Score: ___/25
___ Min.	___ Min.	___ Min.	___ Min.	___ Min.
___ Sec.	___ Sec.	___ Sec.	___ Sec.	___ Sec.

Dividing by Four Review Test

Name: _____

A									
$4\overline{)36}$	$4\overline{)4}$	$4\overline{)8}$	$4\overline{)12}$	$4\overline{)24}$	$4\overline{)16}$	$4\overline{)28}$	$4\overline{)20}$	$4\overline{)32}$	$4\overline{)4}$

B									
$4\overline{)20}$	$4\overline{)12}$	$4\overline{)4}$	$4\overline{)38}$	$4\overline{)32}$	$4\overline{)24}$	$4\overline{)20}$	$4\overline{)16}$	$4\overline{)12}$	$4\overline{)8}$

C									
$4\overline{)16}$	$4\overline{)24}$	$4\overline{)4}$	$4\overline{)8}$	$4\overline{)32}$	$4\overline{)16}$	$4\overline{)20}$	$4\overline{)12}$	$4\overline{)16}$	$4\overline{)8}$

D									
$4\overline{)12}$	$4\overline{)32}$	$4\overline{)8}$	$4\overline{)28}$	$4\overline{)20}$	$4\overline{)16}$	$4\overline{)24}$	$4\overline{)32}$	$4\overline{)36}$	$4\overline{)12}$

E									
$4\overline{)16}$	$4\overline{)4}$	$4\overline{)24}$	$4\overline{)8}$	$4\overline{)28}$	$4\overline{)12}$	$4\overline{)32}$	$4\overline{)16}$	$4\overline{)36}$	$4\overline{)20}$

F									
$4\overline{)4}$	$4\overline{)8}$	$4\overline{)12}$	$4\overline{)16}$	$4\overline{)20}$	$4\overline{)24}$	$4\overline{)16}$	$4\overline{)8}$	$4\overline{)12}$	$4\overline{)4}$

G									
$4\overline{)12}$	$4\overline{)4}$	$4\overline{)16}$	$4\overline{)8}$	$4\overline{)20}$	$4\overline{)28}$	$4\overline{)24}$	$4\overline{)32}$	$4\overline{)36}$	$4\overline{)12}$

H									
$4\overline{)24}$	$4\overline{)20}$	$4\overline{)32}$	$4\overline{)36}$	$4\overline{)16}$	$4\overline{)12}$	$4\overline{)8}$	$4\overline{)4}$	$4\overline{)28}$	$4\overline{)4}$

I									
$4\overline{)8}$	$4\overline{)24}$	$4\overline{)16}$	$4\overline{)12}$	$4\overline{)32}$	$4\overline{)28}$	$4\overline{)12}$	$4\overline{)4}$	$4\overline{)36}$	$4\overline{)12}$

J									
$4\overline{)12}$	$4\overline{)20}$	$4\overline{)32}$	$4\overline{)24}$	$4\overline{)36}$	$4\overline{)28}$	$4\overline{)16}$	$4\overline{)12}$	$4\overline{)8}$	$4\overline{)4}$

Date: _____   Score: _____/100   Time: _____ Min. _____ Sec.

Dividing by Five Drills

Name: _____

Date: Monday _____		Score: ____ /25	Time: ____ Min. ____ Sec.	
5 ÷ 5 = ____	15 ÷ 5 = ____	30 ÷ 5 = ____	25 ÷ 5 = ____	45 ÷ 5 = ____
30 ÷ 5 = ____	25 ÷ 5 = ____	45 ÷ 5 = ____	40 ÷ 5 = ____	10 ÷ 5 = ____
45 ÷ 5 = ____	40 ÷ 5 = ____	10 ÷ 5 = ____	20 ÷ 5 = ____	35 ÷ 5 = ____
10 ÷ 5 = ____	20 ÷ 5 = ____	35 ÷ 5 = ____	5 ÷ 5 = ____	15 ÷ 5 = ____
35 ÷ 5 = ____	5 ÷ 5 = ____	15 ÷ 5 = ____	30 ÷ 5 = ____	25 ÷ 5 = ____

Date: Tuesday _____		Score: ____ /25	Time: ____ Min. ____ Sec.	
40 ÷ 5 = ____	10 ÷ 5 = ____	20 ÷ 5 = ____	35 ÷ 5 = ____	5 ÷ 5 = ____
20 ÷ 5 = ____	35 ÷ 5 = ____	5 ÷ 5 = ____	15 ÷ 5 = ____	30 ÷ 5 = ____
5 ÷ 5 = ____	15 ÷ 5 = ____	30 ÷ 5 = ____	25 ÷ 5 = ____	45 ÷ 5 = ____
30 ÷ 5 = ____	25 ÷ 5 = ____	45 ÷ 5 = ____	40 ÷ 5 = ____	10 ÷ 5 = ____
45 ÷ 5 = ____	40 ÷ 5 = ____	10 ÷ 5 = ____	20 ÷ 5 = ____	35 ÷ 5 = ____

Date: Wednesday _____		Score: ____ /25	Time: ____ Min. ____ Sec.	
15 ÷ 5 = ____	30 ÷ 5 = ____	25 ÷ 5 = ____	45 ÷ 5 = ____	40 ÷ 5 = ____
25 ÷ 5 = ____	45 ÷ 5 = ____	40 ÷ 5 = ____	10 ÷ 5 = ____	20 ÷ 5 = ____
40 ÷ 5 = ____	10 ÷ 5 = ____	20 ÷ 5 = ____	35 ÷ 5 = ____	5 ÷ 5 = ____
20 ÷ 5 = ____	35 ÷ 5 = ____	5 ÷ 5 = ____	15 ÷ 5 = ____	30 ÷ 5 = ____
5 ÷ 5 = ____	15 ÷ 5 = ____	30 ÷ 5 = ____	25 ÷ 5 = ____	45 ÷ 5 = ____

Date: Thursday _____		Score: ____ /25	Time: ____ Min. ____ Sec.	
10 ÷ 5 = ____	20 ÷ 5 = ____	35 ÷ 5 = ____	5 ÷ 5 = ____	15 ÷ 5 = ____
35 ÷ 5 = ____	5 ÷ 5 = ____	15 ÷ 5 = ____	30 ÷ 5 = ____	25 ÷ 5 = ____
15 ÷ 5 = ____	30 ÷ 5 = ____	25 ÷ 5 = ____	45 ÷ 5 = ____	40 ÷ 5 = ____
25 ÷ 5 = ____	45 ÷ 5 = ____	40 ÷ 5 = ____	10 ÷ 5 = ____	20 ÷ 5 = ____
40 ÷ 5 = ____	10 ÷ 5 = ____	20 ÷ 5 = ____	35 ÷ 5 = ____	5 ÷ 5 = ____

Date: Friday _____		Score: ____ /25	Time: ____ Min. ____ Sec.	
30 ÷ 5 = ____	25 ÷ 5 = ____	45 ÷ 5 = ____	40 ÷ 5 = ____	10 ÷ 5 = ____
45 ÷ 5 = ____	40 ÷ 5 = ____	10 ÷ 5 = ____	20 ÷ 5 = ____	35 ÷ 5 = ____
10 ÷ 5 = ____	20 ÷ 5 = ____	35 ÷ 5 = ____	5 ÷ 5 = ____	15 ÷ 5 = ____
35 ÷ 5 = ____	5 ÷ 5 = ____	15 ÷ 5 = ____	30 ÷ 5 = ____	25 ÷ 5 = ____
15 ÷ 5 = ____	30 ÷ 5 = ____	25 ÷ 5 = ____	45 ÷ 5 = ____	40 ÷ 5 = ____

Home Practice Dividing by Five Drills

Name: _____

Monday	Tuesday	Wednesday	Thursday	Friday
40 ÷ 5 = ____	15 ÷ 5 = ____	5 ÷ 5 = ____	30 ÷ 5 = ____	10 ÷ 5 = ____
20 ÷ 5 = ____	25 ÷ 5 = ____	30 ÷ 5 = ____	45 ÷ 5 = ____	35 ÷ 5 = ____
5 ÷ 5 = ____	40 ÷ 5 = ____	45 ÷ 5 = ____	10 ÷ 5 = ____	15 ÷ 5 = ____
30 ÷ 5 = ____	20 ÷ 5 = ____	10 ÷ 5 = ____	35 ÷ 5 = ____	25 ÷ 5 = ____
45 ÷ 5 = ____	5 ÷ 5 = ____	35 ÷ 5 = ____	15 ÷ 5 = ____	40 ÷ 5 = ____
10 ÷ 5 = ____	30 ÷ 5 = ____	15 ÷ 5 = ____	25 ÷ 5 = ____	20 ÷ 5 = ____
35 ÷ 5 = ____	45 ÷ 5 = ____	25 ÷ 5 = ____	40 ÷ 5 = ____	5 ÷ 5 = ____
15 ÷ 5 = ____	10 ÷ 5 = ____	40 ÷ 5 = ____	20 ÷ 5 = ____	30 ÷ 5 = ____
25 ÷ 5 = ____	35 ÷ 5 = ____	20 ÷ 5 = ____	5 ÷ 5 = ____	45 ÷ 5 = ____
40 ÷ 5 = ____	15 ÷ 5 = ____	5 ÷ 5 = ____	30 ÷ 5 = ____	10 ÷ 5 = ____
20 ÷ 5 = ____	25 ÷ 5 = ____	30 ÷ 5 = ____	45 ÷ 5 = ____	35 ÷ 5 = ____
5 ÷ 5 = ____	40 ÷ 5 = ____	45 ÷ 5 = ____	10 ÷ 5 = ____	15 ÷ 5 = ____
30 ÷ 5 = ____	20 ÷ 5 = ____	10 ÷ 5 = ____	35 ÷ 5 = ____	25 ÷ 5 = ____
45 ÷ 5 = ____	5 ÷ 5 = ____	35 ÷ 5 = ____	15 ÷ 5 = ____	40 ÷ 5 = ____
10 ÷ 5 = ____	30 ÷ 5 = ____	15 ÷ 5 = ____	25 ÷ 5 = ____	20 ÷ 5 = ____
35 ÷ 5 = ____	45 ÷ 5 = ____	25 ÷ 5 = ____	40 ÷ 5 = ____	5 ÷ 5 = ____
15 ÷ 5 = ____	10 ÷ 5 = ____	40 ÷ 5 = ____	20 ÷ 5 = ____	30 ÷ 5 = ____
25 ÷ 5 = ____	35 ÷ 5 = ____	20 ÷ 5 = ____	5 ÷ 5 = ____	45 ÷ 5 = ____
40 ÷ 5 = ____	15 ÷ 5 = ____	5 ÷ 5 = ____	30 ÷ 5 = ____	10 ÷ 5 = ____
20 ÷ 5 = ____	25 ÷ 5 = ____	30 ÷ 5 = ____	45 ÷ 5 = ____	35 ÷ 5 = ____
5 ÷ 5 = ____	40 ÷ 5 = ____	45 ÷ 5 = ____	10 ÷ 5 = ____	15 ÷ 5 = ____
30 ÷ 5 = ____	20 ÷ 5 = ____	10 ÷ 5 = ____	35 ÷ 5 = ____	25 ÷ 5 = ____
45 ÷ 5 = ____	5 ÷ 5 = ____	35 ÷ 5 = ____	15 ÷ 5 = ____	40 ÷ 5 = ____
10 ÷ 5 = ____	30 ÷ 5 = ____	15 ÷ 5 = ____	25 ÷ 5 = ____	20 ÷ 5 = ____
35 ÷ 5 = ____	45 ÷ 5 = ____	25 ÷ 5 = ____	40 ÷ 5 = ____	5 ÷ 5 = ____
Score: ____/25 ____ Min. ____ Sec.	Score: ____/25 ____ Min. ____ Sec.	Score: ____/25 ____ Min. ____ Sec.	Score: ____/25 ____ Min. ____ Sec.	Score: ____/25 ____ Min. ____ Sec.

Extra Practice Dividing by Five Drills

Name: _____

Day 1	Day 2	Day 3	Day 4	Day 5
$5 \div \underline{} = 1$	$40 \div \underline{} = 8$	$\underline{} \div 5 = 9$	$35 \div 5 = \underline{}$	$25 \div 5 = \underline{}$
$\underline{} \div 5 = 6$	$\underline{} \div 5 = 3$	$\underline{} \div 5 = 5$	$20 \div 5 = \underline{}$	$45 \div 5 = \underline{}$
$10 \div 5 = \underline{}$	$5 \div 5 = \underline{}$	$\underline{} \div 5 = 8$	$45 \div 5 = \underline{}$	$20 \div 5 = \underline{}$
$35 \div \underline{} = 7$	$30 \div \underline{} = 6$	$\underline{} \div 5 = 3$	$25 \div 5 = \underline{}$	$\underline{} \div 5 = 7$
$\underline{} \div 5 = 4$	$\underline{} \div 5 = 2$	$\underline{} \div 5 = 1$	$40 \div 5 = \underline{}$	$\underline{} \div 5 = 2$
$45 \div 5 = \underline{}$	$35 \div 5 = \underline{}$	$\underline{} \div 5 = 6$	$15 \div 5 = \underline{}$	$\underline{} \div 5 = 6$
$25 \div \underline{} = 5$	$\underline{} \div 5 = 4$	$\underline{} \div 5 = 2$	$5 \div 5 = \underline{}$	$\underline{} \div 5 = 1$
$\underline{} \div 5 = 8$	$45 \div \underline{} = 9$	$\underline{} \div 5 = 7$	$30 \div 5 = \underline{}$	$\underline{} \div 5 = 3$
$15 \div 5 = \underline{}$	$25 \div 5 = \underline{}$	$\underline{} \div 5 = 4$	$10 \div 5 = \underline{}$	$\underline{} \div 5 = 8$
$30 \div \underline{} = 6$	$15 \div \underline{} = 3$	$\underline{} \div 5 = 9$	$35 \div 5 = \underline{}$	$20 \div 5 = \underline{}$
$\underline{} \div 5 = 1$	$\underline{} \div 5 = 8$	$\underline{} \div 5 = 5$	$20 \div 5 = \underline{}$	$40 \div 5 = \underline{}$
$35 \div \underline{} = 7$	$30 \div 5 = \underline{}$	$\underline{} \div 5 = 8$	$45 \div 5 = \underline{}$	$25 \div 5 = \underline{}$
$\underline{} \div 5 = 2$	$5 \div \underline{} = 1$	$\underline{} \div 5 = 3$	$25 \div 5 = \underline{}$	$\underline{} \div 5 = 7$
$20 \div 5 = \underline{}$	$\underline{} \div 5 = 2$	$\underline{} \div 5 = 1$	$40 \div 5 = \underline{}$	$\underline{} \div 5 = 2$
$45 \div \underline{} = 9$	$35 \div 5 = \underline{}$	$\underline{} \div 5 = 6$	$15 \div 5 = \underline{}$	$\underline{} \div 5 = 6$
$\underline{} \div 5 = 5$	$20 \div \underline{} = 4$	$\underline{} \div 5 = 2$	$5 \div 5 = \underline{}$	$\underline{} \div 5 = 1$
$40 \div 5 = \underline{}$	$\underline{} \div 5 = 9$	$\underline{} \div 5 = 7$	$30 \div 5 = \underline{}$	$\underline{} \div 5 = 3$
$15 \div \underline{} = 3$	$25 \div 5 = \underline{}$	$\underline{} \div 5 = 4$	$10 \div 5 = \underline{}$	$\underline{} \div 5 = 8$
$\underline{} \div 5 = 1$	$40 \div \underline{} = 8$	$\underline{} \div 5 = 9$	$35 \div 5 = \underline{}$	$5 \div 5 = \underline{}$
$30 \div 5 = \underline{}$	$\underline{} \div 5 = 3$	$\underline{} \div 5 = 5$	$20 \div 5 = \underline{}$	$30 \div 5 = \underline{}$
$10 \div \underline{} = 2$	$5 \div 5 = \underline{}$	$\underline{} \div 5 = 8$	$45 \div 5 = \underline{}$	$10 \div 5 = \underline{}$
$\underline{} \div 5 = 7$	$30 \div \underline{} = 6$	$\underline{} \div 5 = 3$	$25 \div 5 = \underline{}$	$\underline{} \div 5 = 7$
$20 \div 5 = \underline{}$	$\underline{} \div 5 = 2$	$\underline{} \div 5 = 1$	$40 \div 5 = \underline{}$	$\underline{} \div 5 = 4$
$45 \div \underline{} = 9$	$35 \div 5 = \underline{}$	$\underline{} \div 5 = 6$	$15 \div 5 = \underline{}$	$\underline{} \div 5 = 9$
$\underline{} \div 5 = 5$	$\underline{} \div 5 = 4$	$\underline{} \div 5 = 2$	$5 \div 5 = \underline{}$	$\underline{} \div 5 = 4$
Score: _____/25	Score: _____/25	Score: _____/25	Score: _____/25	Score: _____/25
_____ Min.	_____ Min.	_____ Min.	_____ Min.	_____ Min.
_____ Sec.	_____ Sec.	_____ Sec.	_____ Sec.	_____ Sec.

OTM-1142 • SSK1-42 Timed Division Facts

Dividing by Five Review Test

Name: _____

A									
5)30	5)35	5)5	5)45	5)10	5)25	5)20	5)40	5)15	5)5

B									
5)10	5)20	5)30	5)25	5)15	5)35	5)5	5)30	5)45	5)40

C									
5)35	5)45	5)10	5)20	5)40	5)15	5)25	5)10	5)30	5)5

D									
5)20	5)25	5)40	5)35	5)15	5)45	5)5	5)30	5)10	5)35

E									
5)45	5)15	5)20	5)25	5)5	5)40	5)10	5)35	5)20	5)30

F									
5)25	5)45	5)40	5)15	5)30	5)35	5)20	5)45	5)5	5)10

G									
5)40	5)15	5)25	5)5	5)10	5)20	5)25	5)30	5)45	5)35

H									
5)15	5)30	5)20	5)40	5)5	5)10	5)35	5)45	5)40	5)25

I									
5)5	5)15	5)10	5)25	5)30	5)25	5)40	5)30	5)10	5)45

J									
5)35	5)20	5)45	5)40	5)15	5)25	5)10	5)35	5)40	5)30

Date: _____   Score: _____/100   Time: _____ Min. _____ Sec.

OTM-1142 • SSK1-42 Timed Division Facts

Timed Drill Review for Dividing by 2, 3, 4, and 5

Name: _____

Row 1	Row 2	Row 3	Row 4
6 ÷ 2 = _____	24 ÷ 3 = _____	30 ÷ 5 = _____	24 ÷ 4 = _____
18 ÷ 3 = _____	28 ÷ 4 = _____	12 ÷ 2 = _____	20 ÷ 5 = _____
4 ÷ 4 = _____	40 ÷ 5 = _____	27 ÷ 3 = _____	8 ÷ 2 = _____
30 ÷ 5 = _____	10 ÷ 2 = _____	12 ÷ 4 = _____	9 ÷ 3 = _____
12 ÷ 2 = _____	12 ÷ 3 = _____	10 ÷ 5 = _____	16 ÷ 4 = _____
27 ÷ 3 = _____	20 ÷ 4 = _____	18 ÷ 2 = _____	45 ÷ 5 = _____
32 ÷ 4 = _____	15 ÷ 5 = _____	6 ÷ 3 = _____	14 ÷ 2 = _____
10 ÷ 5 = _____	16 ÷ 2 = _____	24 ÷ 4 = _____	15 ÷ 3 = _____
18 ÷ 2 = _____	3 ÷ 3 = _____	35 ÷ 5 = _____	28 ÷ 4 = _____
6 ÷ 3 = _____	4 ÷ 4 = _____	2 ÷ 2 = _____	25 ÷ 5 = _____
36 ÷ 4 = _____	5 ÷ 5 = _____	21 ÷ 3 = _____	4 ÷ 2 = _____
35 ÷ 5 = _____	6 ÷ 2 = _____	16 ÷ 4 = _____	24 ÷ 3 = _____
2 ÷ 2 = _____	18 ÷ 3 = _____	20 ÷ 5 = _____	20 ÷ 4 = _____
21 ÷ 3 = _____	32 ÷ 4 = _____	2 ÷ 2 = _____	40 ÷ 5 = _____
12 ÷ 4 = _____	30 ÷ 5 = _____	9 ÷ 3 = _____	10 ÷ 2 = _____
20 ÷ 5 = _____	12 ÷ 2 = _____	28 ÷ 4 = _____	12 ÷ 3 = _____
8 ÷ 2 = _____	27 ÷ 3 = _____	45 ÷ 5 = _____	4 ÷ 4 = _____
9 ÷ 3 = _____	36 ÷ 4 = _____	8 ÷ 2 = _____	15 ÷ 5 = _____
24 ÷ 4 = _____	10 ÷ 5 = _____	15 ÷ 3 = _____	16 ÷ 2 = _____
45 ÷ 5 = _____	18 ÷ 2 = _____	20 ÷ 4 = _____	3 ÷ 3 = _____
14 ÷ 2 = _____	6 ÷ 3 = _____	25 ÷ 5 = _____	32 ÷ 4 = _____
15 ÷ 3 = _____	12 ÷ 4 = _____	14 ÷ 2 = _____	5 ÷ 5 = _____
16 ÷ 4 = _____	35 ÷ 5 = _____	24 ÷ 3 = _____	6 ÷ 2 = _____
25 ÷ 5 = _____	2 ÷ 2 = _____	36 ÷ 4 = _____	18 ÷ 2 = _____
4 ÷ 2 = _____	21 ÷ 3 = _____	40 ÷ 5 = _____	36 ÷ 4 = _____

Date: _____ Score: _____/100 Time: _____ Min. _____ Sec.

© On The Mark Press • S&S Learning Materials   OTM-1142 • SSK1-42 Timed Division Facts

Name: _____

A									
2) 6	3) 18	4) 4	5) 30	2) 12	3) 27	4) 32	5) 10	2) 18	3) 6

B									
4) 36	5) 35	2) 2	3) 21	4) 12	5) 20	2) 8	3) 9	4) 24	5) 45

C									
2) 14	3) 15	4) 16	5) 25	2) 4	3) 24	4) 28	5) 40	2) 10	3) 12

D									
4) 20	5) 15	2) 16	3) 3	4) 4	5) 5	2) 6	3) 18	4) 32	5) 30

E									
2) 12	3) 27	4) 36	5) 10	2) 18	3) 6	4) 12	5) 35	2) 2	3) 21

F									
5) 30	2) 12	3) 27	4) 12	5) 10	2) 18	3) 6	4) 24	5) 35	2) 2

G									
3) 21	4) 16	5) 20	2) 2	3) 9	4) 28	5) 45	2) 8	3) 15	4) 20

H									
5) 25	2) 14	3) 24	4) 36	5) 40	4) 24	5) 20	2) 8	3) 9	4) 16

I									
5) 45	2) 14	3) 15	4) 28	5) 25	2) 4	3) 24	4) 20	5) 40	2) 10

J									
3) 12	4) 4	5) 15	2) 16	3) 3	4) 32	5) 5	2) 6	3) 18	4) 36

Date: _____ Score: _____/100 Time: _____ Min. _____ Sec.

Dividing by Six Drills

Name: _____

Date: Monday _____ Score: _____ /25 Time: _____ Min. _____ Sec.

$6 \div 6 =$ ____	$48 \div 6 =$ ____	$24 \div 6 =$ ____	$18 \div 6 =$ ____	$42 \div 6 =$ ____
$24 \div 6 =$ ____	$18 \div 6 =$ ____	$42 \div 6 =$ ____	$54 \div 6 =$ ____	$12 \div 6 =$ ____
$42 \div 6 =$ ____	$54 \div 6 =$ ____	$12 \div 6 =$ ____	$36 \div 6 =$ ____	$30 \div 6 =$ ____
$12 \div 6 =$ ____	$36 \div 6 =$ ____	$30 \div 6 =$ ____	$36 \div 6 =$ ____	$48 \div 6 =$ ____
$30 \div 6 =$ ____	$6 \div 6 =$ ____	$48 \div 6 =$ ____	$24 \div 6 =$ ____	$18 \div 6 =$ ____

Date: Tuesday _____ Score: _____ /25 Time: _____ Min. _____ Sec.

$54 \div 6 =$ ____	$12 \div 6 =$ ____	$36 \div 6 =$ ____	$30 \div 6 =$ ____	$6 \div 6 =$ ____
$36 \div 6 =$ ____	$30 \div 6 =$ ____	$6 \div 6 =$ ____	$48 \div 6 =$ ____	$24 \div 6 =$ ____
$6 \div 6 =$ ____	$48 \div 6 =$ ____	$24 \div 6 =$ ____	$18 \div 6 =$ ____	$42 \div 6 =$ ____
$24 \div 6 =$ ____	$18 \div 6 =$ ____	$42 \div 6 =$ ____	$54 \div 6 =$ ____	$12 \div 6 =$ ____
$42 \div 6 =$ ____	$54 \div 6 =$ ____	$12 \div 6 =$ ____	$36 \div 6 =$ ____	$30 \div 6 =$ ____

Date: Wednesday _____ Score: _____ /25 Time: _____ Min. _____ Sec.

$48 \div 6 =$ ____	$24 \div 6 =$ ____	$18 \div 6 =$ ____	$42 \div 6 =$ ____	$54 \div 6 =$ ____
$18 \div 6 =$ ____	$42 \div 6 =$ ____	$54 \div 6 =$ ____	$12 \div 6 =$ ____	$36 \div 6 =$ ____
$54 \div 6 =$ ____	$12 \div 6 =$ ____	$36 \div 6 =$ ____	$30 \div 6 =$ ____	$6 \div 6 =$ ____
$36 \div 6 =$ ____	$30 \div 6 =$ ____	$6 \div 6 =$ ____	$48 \div 6 =$ ____	$24 \div 6 =$ ____
$6 \div 6 =$ ____	$48 \div 6 =$ ____	$24 \div 6 =$ ____	$18 \div 6 =$ ____	$42 \div 6 =$ ____

Date: Thursday _____ Score: _____ /25 Time: _____ Min. _____ Sec.

$12 \div 6 =$ ____	$36 \div 6 =$ ____	$30 \div 6 =$ ____	$6 \div 6 =$ ____	$48 \div 6 =$ ____
$30 \div 6 =$ ____	$6 \div 6 =$ ____	$48 \div 6 =$ ____	$24 \div 6 =$ ____	$18 \div 6 =$ ____
$48 \div 6 =$ ____	$24 \div 6 =$ ____	$18 \div 6 =$ ____	$42 \div 6 =$ ____	$54 \div 6 =$ ____
$18 \div 6 =$ ____	$42 \div 6 =$ ____	$54 \div 6 =$ ____	$12 \div 6 =$ ____	$36 \div 6 =$ ____
$54 \div 6 =$ ____	$12 \div 6 =$ ____	$36 \div 6 =$ ____	$30 \div 6 =$ ____	$6 \div 6 =$ ____

Date: Friday _____ Score: _____ /25 Time: _____ Min. _____ Sec.

$24 \div 6 =$ ____	$18 \div 6 =$ ____	$42 \div 6 =$ ____	$54 \div 6 =$ ____	$12 \div 6 =$ ____
$42 \div 6 =$ ____	$54 \div 6 =$ ____	$12 \div 6 =$ ____	$36 \div 6 =$ ____	$30 \div 6 =$ ____
$12 \div 6 =$ ____	$36 \div 6 =$ ____	$30 \div 6 =$ ____	$6 \div 6 =$ ____	$48 \div 6 =$ ____
$30 \div 6 =$ ____	$6 \div 6 =$ ____	$48 \div 6 =$ ____	$24 \div 6 =$ ____	$18 \div 6 =$ ____
$48 \div 6 =$ ____	$24 \div 6 =$ ____	$18 \div 6 =$ ____	$42 \div 6 =$ ____	$54 \div 6 =$ ____

Home Practice Dividing by Six Drills

Name: _____

Monday	Tuesday	Wednesday	Thursday	Friday
6 ÷ 6 = ____	54 ÷ 6 = ____	12 ÷ 6 = ____	48 ÷ 6 = ____	24 ÷ 6 = ____
24 ÷ 6 = ____	36 ÷ 6 = ____	30 ÷ 6 = ____	18 ÷ 6 = ____	42 ÷ 6 = ____
42 ÷ 6 = ____	6 ÷ 6 = ____	48 ÷ 6 = ____	54 ÷ 6 = ____	12 ÷ 6 = ____
12 ÷ 6 = ____	24 ÷ 6 = ____	18 ÷ 6 = ____	36 ÷ 6 = ____	30 ÷ 6 = ____
30 ÷ 6 = ____	42 ÷ 6 = ____	54 ÷ 6 = ____	6 ÷ 6 = ____	48 ÷ 6 = ____
48 ÷ 6 = ____	12 ÷ 6 = ____	36 ÷ 6 = ____	24 ÷ 6 = ____	18 ÷ 6 = ____
18 ÷ 6 = ____	30 ÷ 6 = ____	6 ÷ 6 = ____	42 ÷ 6 = ____	54 ÷ 6 = ____
54 ÷ 6 = ____	48 ÷ 6 = ____	24 ÷ 6 = ____	12 ÷ 6 = ____	36 ÷ 6 = ____
36 ÷ 6 = ____	18 ÷ 6 = ____	42 ÷ 6 = ____	30 ÷ 6 = ____	6 ÷ 6 = ____
6 ÷ 6 = ____	54 ÷ 6 = ____	12 ÷ 6 = ____	48 ÷ 6 = ____	24 ÷ 6 = ____
24 ÷ 6 = ____	36 ÷ 6 = ____	30 ÷ 6 = ____	18 ÷ 6 = ____	42 ÷ 6 = ____
42 ÷ 6 = ____	6 ÷ 6 = ____	48 ÷ 6 = ____	54 ÷ 6 = ____	12 ÷ 6 = ____
12 ÷ 6 = ____	24 ÷ 6 = ____	18 ÷ 6 = ____	36 ÷ 6 = ____	30 ÷ 6 = ____
30 ÷ 6 = ____	42 ÷ 6 = ____	54 ÷ 6 = ____	6 ÷ 6 = ____	48 ÷ 6 = ____
48 ÷ 6 = ____	12 ÷ 6 = ____	36 ÷ 6 = ____	24 ÷ 6 = ____	18 ÷ 6 = ____
18 ÷ 6 = ____	30 ÷ 6 = ____	6 ÷ 6 = ____	42 ÷ 6 = ____	54 ÷ 6 = ____
54 ÷ 6 = ____	48 ÷ 6 = ____	24 ÷ 6 = ____	12 ÷ 6 = ____	36 ÷ 6 = ____
36 ÷ 6 = ____	18 ÷ 6 = ____	42 ÷ 6 = ____	30 ÷ 6 = ____	6 ÷ 6 = ____
6 ÷ 6 = ____	54 ÷ 6 = ____	12 ÷ 6 = ____	48 ÷ 6 = ____	24 ÷ 6 = ____
24 ÷ 6 = ____	36 ÷ 6 = ____	30 ÷ 6 = ____	18 ÷ 6 = ____	42 ÷ 6 = ____
42 ÷ 6 = ____	6 ÷ 6 = ____	48 ÷ 6 = ____	54 ÷ 6 = ____	12 ÷ 6 = ____
12 ÷ 6 = ____	24 ÷ 6 = ____	18 ÷ 6 = ____	36 ÷ 6 = ____	30 ÷ 6 = ____
30 ÷ 6 = ____	42 ÷ 6 = ____	54 ÷ 6 = ____	6 ÷ 6 = ____	48 ÷ 6 = ____
48 ÷ 6 = ____	12 ÷ 6 = ____	36 ÷ 6 = ____	24 ÷ 6 = ____	18 ÷ 6 = ____
18 ÷ 6 = ____	30 ÷ 6 = ____	6 ÷ 6 = ____	42 ÷ 6 = ____	54 ÷ 6 = ____
Score: ____/25 ____ Min. ____ Sec.	Score: ____/25 ____ Min. ____ Sec.	Score: ____/25 ____ Min. ____ Sec.	Score: ____/25 ____ Min. ____ Sec.	Score: ____/25 ____ Min. ____ Sec.

Extra Practice Dividing by Six Drills

Name: _____

Day 1	Day 2	Day 3	Day 4	Day 5
6 ÷ ___ = 1	18 ÷ ___ = 3	___ ÷ 6 = 1	54 ÷ 6 = ___	12 ÷ 6 = ___
___ ÷ 6 = 4	___ ÷ 6 = 7	___ ÷ 6 = 4	36 ÷ 6 = ___	30 ÷ 6 = ___
48 ÷ 6 = ___	6 ÷ 6 = ___	___ ÷ 6 = 8	18 ÷ 6 = ___	54 ÷ 6 = ___
12 ÷ ___ = 2	24 ÷ ___ = 4	___ ÷ 6 = 2	42 ÷ 6 = ___	___ ÷ 6 = 6
___ ÷ 6 = 5	___ ÷ 6 = 8	___ ÷ 6 = 5	6 ÷ 6 = ___	___ ÷ 6 = 8
54 ÷ 6 = ___	12 ÷ 6 = ___	___ ÷ 6 = 9	24 ÷ 6 = ___	___ ÷ 6 = 1
36 ÷ ___ = 6	30 ÷ ___ = 5	___ ÷ 6 = 6	48 ÷ 6 = ___	___ ÷ 6 = 4
___ ÷ 6 = 3	___ ÷ 6 = 9	___ ÷ 6 = 3	12 ÷ 6 = ___	___ ÷ 6 = 8
42 ÷ 6 = ___	36 ÷ 6 = ___	___ ÷ 6 = 7	30 ÷ 6 = ___	___ ÷ 6 = 2
24 ÷ ___ = 4	18 ÷ ___ = 3	___ ÷ 6 = 1	54 ÷ 6 = ___	30 ÷ 6 = ___
___ ÷ 6 = 8	___ ÷ 6 = 7	___ ÷ 6 = 4	36 ÷ 6 = ___	54 ÷ 6 = ___
6 ÷ 6 = ___	6 ÷ 6 = ___	___ ÷ 6 = 8	18 ÷ 6 = ___	36 ÷ 6 = ___
12 ÷ ___ = 2	24 ÷ ___ = 4	___ ÷ 6 = 2	42 ÷ 6 = ___	___ ÷ 6 = 3
___ ÷ 6 = 5	___ ÷ 6 = 8	___ ÷ 6 = 5	6 ÷ 6 = ___	___ ÷ 6 = 8
54 ÷ 6 = ___	12 ÷ 6 = ___	___ ÷ 6 = 9	24 ÷ 6 = ___	___ ÷ 6 = 1
18 ÷ ___ = 3	30 ÷ ___ = 5	___ ÷ 6 = 6	48 ÷ 6 = ___	___ ÷ 6 = 3
___ ÷ 6 = 9	___ ÷ 6 = 9	___ ÷ 6 = 3	12 ÷ 6 = ___	___ ÷ 6 = 8
36 ÷ 6 = ___	36 ÷ 6 = ___	___ ÷ 6 = 8	30 ÷ 6 = ___	___ ÷ 6 = 2
42 ÷ ___ = 7	42 ÷ ___ = 7	___ ÷ 6 = 1	54 ÷ 6 = ___	30 ÷ 6 = ___
___ ÷ 6 = 1	___ ÷ 6 = 3	___ ÷ 6 = 4	36 ÷ 6 = ___	54 ÷ 6 = ___
24 ÷ 6 = ___	24 ÷ 6 = ___	___ ÷ 6 = 8	18 ÷ 6 = ___	36 ÷ 6 = ___
48 ÷ ___ = 8	6 ÷ ___ = 1	___ ÷ 6 = 2	42 ÷ 6 = ___	___ ÷ 6 = 3
___ ÷ 6 = 2	___ ÷ 6 = 4	___ ÷ 6 = 5	6 ÷ 6 = ___	___ ÷ 6 = 7
30 ÷ 6 = ___	48 ÷ 6 = ___	___ ÷ 6 = 9	24 ÷ 6 = ___	___ ÷ 6 = 8
54 ÷ ___ = 9	12 ÷ ___ = 2	___ ÷ 6 = 6	48 ÷ 6 = ___	___ ÷ 6 = 9
Score: _____/25	Score: _____/25	Score: _____/25	Score: _____/25	Score: _____/25
_____ Min.	_____ Min.	_____ Min.	_____ Min.	_____ Min.
_____ Sec.	_____ Sec.	_____ Sec.	_____ Sec.	_____ Sec.

Dividing by Six Review Test

Name: _____

A									
6)‾6̅	6)‾2̅4̅	6)‾1̅8̅	6)‾1̅2̅	6)‾3̅0̅	6)‾5̅4̅	6)‾3̅6̅	6)‾1̅8̅	6)‾4̅2̅	6)‾6̅

B									
6)‾2̅4̅	6)‾4̅8̅	6)‾1̅2̅	6)‾3̅0̅	6)‾5̅4̅	6)‾3̅6̅	6)‾1̅8̅	6)‾4̅2̅	6)‾6̅	6)‾2̅4̅

C									
6)‾4̅8̅	6)‾1̅2̅	6)‾3̅0̅	6)‾5̅4̅	6)‾3̅6̅	6)‾1̅8̅	6)‾4̅2̅	6)‾6̅	6)‾2̅4̅	6)‾1̅2̅

D									
6)‾4̅8̅	6)‾3̅0̅	6)‾2̅4̅	6)‾1̅2̅	6)‾5̅4̅	6)‾3̅6̅	6)‾1̅8̅	6)‾4̅2̅	6)‾6̅	6)‾2̅4̅

E									
6)‾1̅2̅	6)‾5̅4̅	6)‾4̅8̅	6)‾3̅0̅	6)‾3̅6̅	6)‾4̅2̅	6)‾6̅	6)‾2̅4̅	6)‾1̅8̅	6)‾4̅8̅

F									
6)‾3̅0̅	6)‾3̅6̅	6)‾1̅2̅	6)‾1̅8̅	6)‾4̅2̅	6)‾6̅	6)‾2̅4̅	6)‾4̅8̅	6)‾1̅2̅	6)‾3̅0̅

G									
6)‾5̅4̅	6)‾1̅8̅	6)‾4̅2̅	6)‾3̅6̅	6)‾2̅4̅	6)‾1̅2̅	6)‾4̅8̅	6)‾6̅	6)‾3̅0̅	6)‾5̅4̅

H									
6)‾3̅6̅	6)‾6̅	6)‾2̅4̅	6)‾1̅8̅	6)‾1̅2̅	6)‾4̅2̅	6)‾4̅8̅	6)‾3̅0̅	6)‾5̅4̅	6)‾3̅6̅

I									
6)‾1̅8̅	6)‾4̅2̅	6)‾6̅	6)‾2̅4̅	6)‾4̅8̅	6)‾1̅2̅	6)‾3̅0̅	6)‾5̅4̅	6)‾1̅8̅	6)‾4̅2̅

J									
6)‾3̅6̅	6)‾5̅4̅	6)‾2̅4̅	6)‾1̅2̅	6)‾6̅	6)‾1̅8̅	6)‾3̅0̅	6)‾4̅8̅	6)‾4̅2̅	6)‾3̅6̅

Date: _____   Score: _____/100   Time: _____ Min. _____ Sec.

Dividing by Seven Drills

Name: _____

Date: Monday _____ Score: _____ /25 Time: _____ Min. _____ Sec.

7 ÷ 7 = ____	56 ÷ 7 = ____	28 ÷ 7 = ____	21 ÷ 7 = ____	49 ÷ 7 = ____
28 ÷ 7 = ____	21 ÷ 7 = ____	49 ÷ 7 = ____	42 ÷ 7 = ____	14 ÷ 7 = ____
49 ÷ 7 = ____	42 ÷ 7 = ____	14 ÷ 7 = ____	63 ÷ 7 = ____	35 ÷ 7 = ____
14 ÷ 7 = ____	63 ÷ 7 = ____	35 ÷ 7 = ____	7 ÷ 7 = ____	56 ÷ 7 = ____
35 ÷ 7 = ____	7 ÷ 7 = ____	56 ÷ 7 = ____	28 ÷ 7 = ____	21 ÷ 7 = ____

Date: Tuesday _____ Score: _____ /25 Time: _____ Min. _____ Sec.

21 ÷ 7 = ____	14 ÷ 7 = ____	63 ÷ 7 = ____	35 ÷ 7 = ____	7 ÷ 7 = ____
63 ÷ 7 = ____	35 ÷ 7 = ____	7 ÷ 7 = ____	56 ÷ 7 = ____	28 ÷ 7 = ____
7 ÷ 7 = ____	56 ÷ 7 = ____	28 ÷ 7 = ____	21 ÷ 7 = ____	49 ÷ 7 = ____
28 ÷ 7 = ____	21 ÷ 7 = ____	49 ÷ 7 = ____	42 ÷ 7 = ____	14 ÷ 7 = ____
49 ÷ 7 = ____	42 ÷ 7 = ____	14 ÷ 7 = ____	63 ÷ 7 = ____	35 ÷ 7 = ____

Date: Wednesday _____ Score: _____ /25 Time: _____ Min. _____ Sec.

56 ÷ 7 = ____	28 ÷ 7 = ____	21 ÷ 7 = ____	49 ÷ 7 = ____	42 ÷ 7 = ____
21 ÷ 7 = ____	49 ÷ 7 = ____	42 ÷ 7 = ____	14 ÷ 7 = ____	63 ÷ 7 = ____
42 ÷ 7 = ____	14 ÷ 7 = ____	63 ÷ 7 = ____	35 ÷ 7 = ____	7 ÷ 7 = ____
63 ÷ 7 = ____	35 ÷ 7 = ____	7 ÷ 7 = ____	56 ÷ 7 = ____	28 ÷ 7 = ____
7 ÷ 7 = ____	56 ÷ 7 = ____	28 ÷ 7 = ____	21 ÷ 7 = ____	49 ÷ 7 = ____

Date: Thursday _____ Score: _____ /25 Time: _____ Min. _____ Sec.

14 ÷ 7 = ____	63 ÷ 7 = ____	35 ÷ 7 = ____	7 ÷ 7 = ____	56 ÷ 7 = ____
35 ÷ 7 = ____	7 ÷ 7 = ____	56 ÷ 7 = ____	28 ÷ 7 = ____	21 ÷ 7 = ____
56 ÷ 7 = ____	28 ÷ 7 = ____	21 ÷ 7 = ____	49 ÷ 7 = ____	42 ÷ 7 = ____
21 ÷ 7 = ____	49 ÷ 7 = ____	42 ÷ 7 = ____	14 ÷ 7 = ____	63 ÷ 7 = ____
42 ÷ 7 = ____	14 ÷ 7 = ____	63 ÷ 7 = ____	35 ÷ 7 = ____	7 ÷ 7 = ____

Date: Friday _____ Score: _____ /25 Time: _____ Min. _____ Sec.

28 ÷ 7 = ____	21 ÷ 7 = ____	49 ÷ 7 = ____	42 ÷ 7 = ____	14 ÷ 7 = ____
49 ÷ 7 = ____	42 ÷ 7 = ____	14 ÷ 7 = ____	63 ÷ 7 = ____	35 ÷ 7 = ____
14 ÷ 7 = ____	63 ÷ 7 = ____	35 ÷ 7 = ____	7 ÷ 7 = ____	56 ÷ 7 = ____
35 ÷ 7 = ____	7 ÷ 7 = ____	56 ÷ 7 = ____	28 ÷ 7 = ____	21 ÷ 7 = ____
56 ÷ 7 = ____	28 ÷ 7 = ____	21 ÷ 7 = ____	49 ÷ 7 = ____	42 ÷ 7 = ____

Home Practice Dividing by Seven Drills

Name: _____

Monday	Tuesday	Wednesday	Thursday	Friday
28 ÷ 7 = ____	14 ÷ 7 = ____	7 ÷ 7 = ____	56 ÷ 7 = ____	42 ÷ 7 = ____
49 ÷ 7 = ____	35 ÷ 7 = ____	28 ÷ 7 = ____	21 ÷ 7 = ____	63 ÷ 7 = ____
14 ÷ 7 = ____	56 ÷ 7 = ____	49 ÷ 7 = ____	42 ÷ 7 = ____	7 ÷ 7 = ____
35 ÷ 7 = ____	21 ÷ 7 = ____	14 ÷ 7 = ____	63 ÷ 7 = ____	28 ÷ 7 = ____
56 ÷ 7 = ____	42 ÷ 7 = ____	35 ÷ 7 = ____	7 ÷ 7 = ____	49 ÷ 7 = ____
21 ÷ 7 = ____	63 ÷ 7 = ____	56 ÷ 7 = ____	28 ÷ 7 = ____	14 ÷ 7 = ____
42 ÷ 7 = ____	7 ÷ 7 = ____	21 ÷ 7 = ____	49 ÷ 7 = ____	35 ÷ 7 = ____
63 ÷ 7 = ____	28 ÷ 7 = ____	42 ÷ 7 = ____	14 ÷ 7 = ____	56 ÷ 7 = ____
7 ÷ 7 = ____	49 ÷ 7 = ____	63 ÷ 7 = ____	35 ÷ 7 = ____	21 ÷ 7 = ____
28 ÷ 7 = ____	14 ÷ 7 = ____	7 ÷ 7 = ____	56 ÷ 7 = ____	42 ÷ 7 = ____
49 ÷ 7 = ____	35 ÷ 7 = ____	28 ÷ 7 = ____	21 ÷ 7 = ____	63 ÷ 7 = ____
14 ÷ 7 = ____	56 ÷ 7 = ____	49 ÷ 7 = ____	42 ÷ 7 = ____	7 ÷ 7 = ____
35 ÷ 7 = ____	21 ÷ 7 = ____	14 ÷ 7 = ____	63 ÷ 7 = ____	28 ÷ 7 = ____
56 ÷ 7 = ____	42 ÷ 7 = ____	35 ÷ 7 = ____	7 ÷ 7 = ____	49 ÷ 7 = ____
21 ÷ 7 = ____	63 ÷ 7 = ____	56 ÷ 7 = ____	28 ÷ 7 = ____	14 ÷ 7 = ____
42 ÷ 7 = ____	7 ÷ 7 = ____	21 ÷ 7 = ____	49 ÷ 7 = ____	35 ÷ 7 = ____
63 ÷ 7 = ____	28 ÷ 7 = ____	42 ÷ 7 = ____	14 ÷ 7 = ____	56 ÷ 7 = ____
7 ÷ 7 = ____	49 ÷ 7 = ____	63 ÷ 7 = ____	35 ÷ 7 = ____	21 ÷ 7 = ____
28 ÷ 7 = ____	14 ÷ 7 = ____	7 ÷ 7 = ____	56 ÷ 7 = ____	42 ÷ 7 = ____
49 ÷ 7 = ____	35 ÷ 7 = ____	28 ÷ 7 = ____	21 ÷ 7 = ____	63 ÷ 7 = ____
14 ÷ 7 = ____	56 ÷ 7 = ____	49 ÷ 7 = ____	42 ÷ 7 = ____	7 ÷ 7 = ____
35 ÷ 7 = ____	21 ÷ 7 = ____	14 ÷ 7 = ____	63 ÷ 7 = ____	28 ÷ 7 = ____
56 ÷ 7 = ____	42 ÷ 7 = ____	35 ÷ 7 = ____	7 ÷ 7 = ____	49 ÷ 7 = ____
21 ÷ 7 = ____	63 ÷ 7 = ____	56 ÷ 7 = ____	28 ÷ 7 = ____	14 ÷ 7 = ____
42 ÷ 7 = ____	7 ÷ 7 = ____	21 ÷ 7 = ____	49 ÷ 7 = ____	35 ÷ 7 = ____
Score: ____ /25 ____ Min. ____ Sec.	Score: ____ /25 ____ Min. ____ Sec.	Score: ____ /25 ____ Min. ____ Sec.	Score: ____ /25 ____ Min. ____ Sec.	Score: ____ /25 ____ Min. ____ Sec.

Extra Practice Dividing by Seven Drills

Name: _____

Day 1	Day 2	Day 3	Day 4	Day 5
56 ÷ ___ = 8	14 ÷ ___ = 2	___ ÷ 7 = 1	42 ÷ 7 = ___	49 ÷ 7 = ___
___ ÷ 7 = 3	___ ÷ 7 = 5	___ ÷ 7 = 4	63 ÷ 7 = ___	28 ÷ 7 = ___
42 ÷ 7 = ___	56 ÷ 7 = ___	___ ÷ 7 = 7	7 ÷ 7 = ___	7 ÷ 7 = ___
63 ÷ ___ = 9	21 ÷ ___ = 3	___ ÷ 7 = 2	28 ÷ 7 = ___	___ ÷ 7 = 9
___ ÷ 7 = 1	___ ÷ 7 = 6	___ ÷ 7 = 5	49 ÷ 7 = ___	___ ÷ 7 = 6
28 ÷ ___ = 4	63 ÷ 7 = ___	___ ÷ 7 = 8	14 ÷ 7 = ___	___ ÷ 7 = 3
___ ÷ 7 = 7	7 ÷ ___ = 1	___ ÷ 7 = 3	35 ÷ 7 = ___	___ ÷ 7 = 8
14 ÷ 7 = ___	___ ÷ 7 = 4	___ ÷ 7 = 6	56 ÷ 7 = ___	___ ÷ 7 = 5
35 ÷ ___ = 5	49 ÷ 7 = ___	___ ÷ 7 = 9	21 ÷ 7 = ___	___ ÷ 7 = 2
___ ÷ 7 = 8	14 ÷ ___ = 2	___ ÷ 7 = 1	42 ÷ 7 = ___	21 ÷ 7 = ___
___ ÷ 7 = 3	35 ÷ 7 = ___	___ ÷ 7 = 4	63 ÷ 7 = ___	56 ÷ 7 = ___
42 ÷ 7 = ___	56 ÷ ___ = 8	___ ÷ 7 = 7	7 ÷ 7 = ___	35 ÷ 7 = ___
7 ÷ ___ = 1	___ ÷ 7 = 3	___ ÷ 7 = 2	28 ÷ 7 = ___	___ ÷ 7 = 4
___ ÷ 7 = 9	42 ÷ 7 = ___	___ ÷ 7 = 5	49 ÷ 7 = ___	___ ÷ 7 = 1
28 ÷ 7 = ___	63 ÷ ___ = 9	___ ÷ 7 = 8	14 ÷ 7 = ___	___ ÷ 7 = 9
49 ÷ ___ = 7	___ ÷ 7 = 1	___ ÷ 7 = 3	35 ÷ 7 = ___	___ ÷ 7 = 6
___ ÷ 7 = 2	28 ÷ 7 = ___	___ ÷ 7 = 6	56 ÷ 7 = ___	___ ÷ 7 = 2
35 ÷ 7 = ___	49 ÷ ___ = 7	___ ÷ 7 = 9	21 ÷ 7 = ___	___ ÷ 7 = 7
21 ÷ ___ = 3	___ ÷ 7 = 2	___ ÷ 7 = 1	42 ÷ 7 = ___	28 ÷ 7 = ___
___ ÷ 7 = 8	35 ÷ 7 = ___	___ ÷ 7 = 4	63 ÷ 7 = ___	7 ÷ 7 = ___
63 ÷ 7 = ___	56 ÷ ___ = 8	___ ÷ 7 = 7	7 ÷ 7 = ___	63 ÷ 7 = ___
42 ÷ ___ = 6	___ ÷ 7 = 3	___ ÷ 7 = 2	28 ÷ 7 = ___	___ ÷ 7 = 6
___ ÷ 7 = 1	42 ÷ 7 = ___	___ ÷ 7 = 5	49 ÷ 7 = ___	___ ÷ 7 = 3
28 ÷ 7 = ___	63 ÷ ___ = 9	___ ÷ 7 = 8	14 ÷ 7 = ___	___ ÷ 7 = 8
49 ÷ ___ = 7	___ ÷ 7 = 1	___ ÷ 7 = 3	35 ÷ 7 = ___	___ ÷ 7 = 9
Score: _____/25	Score: _____/25	Score: _____/25	Score: _____/25	Score: _____/25
_____ Min.	_____ Min.	_____ Min.	_____ Min.	_____ Min.
_____ Sec.	_____ Sec.	_____ Sec.	_____ Sec.	_____ Sec.

Dividing by Seven Review Test

Name: _____

A

$7)\overline{56}$ $7)\overline{21}$ $7)\overline{42}$ $7)\overline{63}$ $7)\overline{7}$ $7)\overline{28}$ $7)\overline{49}$ $7)\overline{14}$ $7)\overline{35}$ $7)\overline{56}$

B

$7)\overline{21}$ $7)\overline{42}$ $7)\overline{63}$ $7)\overline{7}$ $7)\overline{28}$ $7)\overline{49}$ $7)\overline{14}$ $7)\overline{35}$ $7)\overline{56}$ $7)\overline{21}$

C

$7)\overline{7}$ $7)\overline{63}$ $7)\overline{7}$ $7)\overline{42}$ $7)\overline{14}$ $7)\overline{35}$ $7)\overline{28}$ $7)\overline{21}$ $7)\overline{42}$ $7)\overline{49}$

D

$7)\overline{63}$ $7)\overline{7}$ $7)\overline{28}$ $7)\overline{49}$ $7)\overline{56}$ $7)\overline{21}$ $7)\overline{42}$ $7)\overline{14}$ $7)\overline{63}$ $7)\overline{35}$

E

$7)\overline{7}$ $7)\overline{63}$ $7)\overline{56}$ $7)\overline{21}$ $7)\overline{42}$ $7)\overline{35}$ $7)\overline{14}$ $7)\overline{49}$ $7)\overline{28}$ $7)\overline{7}$

F

$7)\overline{28}$ $7)\overline{49}$ $7)\overline{14}$ $7)\overline{35}$ $7)\overline{56}$ $7)\overline{21}$ $7)\overline{42}$ $7)\overline{63}$ $7)\overline{7}$ $7)\overline{28}$

G

$7)\overline{49}$ $7)\overline{28}$ $7)\overline{7}$ $7)\overline{63}$ $7)\overline{21}$ $7)\overline{42}$ $7)\overline{56}$ $7)\overline{35}$ $7)\overline{14}$ $7)\overline{49}$

H

$7)\overline{28}$ $7)\overline{7}$ $7)\overline{63}$ $7)\overline{42}$ $7)\overline{21}$ $7)\overline{56}$ $7)\overline{35}$ $7)\overline{14}$ $7)\overline{49}$ $7)\overline{28}$

I

$7)\overline{7}$ $7)\overline{28}$ $7)\overline{49}$ $7)\overline{14}$ $7)\overline{56}$ $7)\overline{35}$ $7)\overline{21}$ $7)\overline{42}$ $7)\overline{63}$ $7)\overline{7}$

J

$7)\overline{42}$ $7)\overline{63}$ $7)\overline{7}$ $7)\overline{28}$ $7)\overline{49}$ $7)\overline{14}$ $7)\overline{35}$ $7)\overline{56}$ $7)\overline{21}$ $7)\overline{42}$

Date: _____   Score: _____/100   Time: _____ Min. _____ Sec.

Dividing by Eight Drills

Name: _____

Date: Monday _____ Score: _____ /25 Time: _____ Min. _____ Sec.

8 ÷ 8 = ____	24 ÷ 8 = ____	40 ÷ 8 = ____	56 ÷ 8 = ____	72 ÷ 8 = ____
40 ÷ 8 = ____	56 ÷ 8 = ____	72 ÷ 8 = ____	32 ÷ 8 = ____	16 ÷ 8 = ____
72 ÷ 8 = ____	32 ÷ 8 = ____	16 ÷ 8 = ____	64 ÷ 8 = ____	48 ÷ 8 = ____
16 ÷ 8 = ____	64 ÷ 8 = ____	48 ÷ 8 = ____	8 ÷ 8 = ____	24 ÷ 8 = ____
48 ÷ 8 = ____	8 ÷ 8 = ____	24 ÷ 8 = ____	40 ÷ 8 = ____	56 ÷ 8 = ____

Date: Tuesday _____ Score: _____ /25 Time: _____ Min. _____ Sec.

32 ÷ 8 = ____	16 ÷ 8 = ____	64 ÷ 8 = ____	48 ÷ 8 = ____	8 ÷ 8 = ____
64 ÷ 8 = ____	48 ÷ 8 = ____	8 ÷ 8 = ____	24 ÷ 8 = ____	40 ÷ 8 = ____
8 ÷ 8 = ____	24 ÷ 8 = ____	40 ÷ 8 = ____	56 ÷ 8 = ____	72 ÷ 8 = ____
40 ÷ 8 = ____	56 ÷ 8 = ____	72 ÷ 8 = ____	32 ÷ 8 = ____	16 ÷ 8 = ____
72 ÷ 8 = ____	32 ÷ 8 = ____	16 ÷ 8 = ____	64 ÷ 8 = ____	48 ÷ 8 = ____

Date: Wednesday _____ Score: _____ /25 Time: _____ Min. _____ Sec.

24 ÷ 8 = ____	40 ÷ 8 = ____	56 ÷ 8 = ____	72 ÷ 8 = ____	32 ÷ 8 = ____
56 ÷ 8 = ____	72 ÷ 8 = ____	32 ÷ 8 = ____	16 ÷ 8 = ____	64 ÷ 8 = ____
32 ÷ 8 = ____	16 ÷ 8 = ____	64 ÷ 8 = ____	48 ÷ 8 = ____	8 ÷ 8 = ____
64 ÷ 8 = ____	48 ÷ 8 = ____	8 ÷ 8 = ____	24 ÷ 8 = ____	40 ÷ 8 = ____
8 ÷ 8 = ____	24 ÷ 8 = ____	40 ÷ 8 = ____	56 ÷ 8 = ____	72 ÷ 8 = ____

Date: Thursday _____ Score: _____ /25 Time: _____ Min. _____ Sec.

16 ÷ 8 = ____	64 ÷ 8 = ____	48 ÷ 8 = ____	8 ÷ 8 = ____	24 ÷ 8 = ____
48 ÷ 8 = ____	8 ÷ 8 = ____	24 ÷ 8 = ____	40 ÷ 8 = ____	56 ÷ 8 = ____
24 ÷ 8 = ____	40 ÷ 8 = ____	56 ÷ 8 = ____	72 ÷ 8 = ____	32 ÷ 8 = ____
56 ÷ 8 = ____	72 ÷ 8 = ____	32 ÷ 8 = ____	16 ÷ 8 = ____	64 ÷ 8 = ____
32 ÷ 8 = ____	16 ÷ 8 = ____	64 ÷ 8 = ____	48 ÷ 8 = ____	8 ÷ 8 = ____

Date: Friday _____ Score: _____ /25 Time: _____ Min. _____ Sec.

40 ÷ 8 = ____	56 ÷ 8 = ____	16 ÷ 8 = ____	64 ÷ 8 = ____	48 ÷ 8 = ____
72 ÷ 8 = ____	32 ÷ 8 = ____	48 ÷ 8 = ____	8 ÷ 8 = ____	24 ÷ 8 = ____
16 ÷ 8 = ____	8 ÷ 8 = ____	24 ÷ 8 = ____	40 ÷ 8 = ____	56 ÷ 8 = ____
48 ÷ 8 = ____	40 ÷ 8 = ____	56 ÷ 8 = ____	72 ÷ 8 = ____	32 ÷ 8 = ____
24 ÷ 8 = ____	72 ÷ 8 = ____	32 ÷ 8 = ____	16 ÷ 8 = ____	64 ÷ 8 = ____

Home Practice Dividing by Eight Drills

Name: _____

Monday	Tuesday	Wednesday	Thursday	Friday
8 ÷ 8 = ____	40 ÷ 8 = ____	32 ÷ 8 = ____	24 ÷ 8 = ____	16 ÷ 8 = ____
40 ÷ 8 = ____	72 ÷ 8 = ____	64 ÷ 8 = ____	56 ÷ 8 = ____	48 ÷ 8 = ____
72 ÷ 8 = ____	16 ÷ 8 = ____	8 ÷ 8 = ____	32 ÷ 8 = ____	24 ÷ 8 = ____
16 ÷ 8 = ____	48 ÷ 8 = ____	40 ÷ 8 = ____	64 ÷ 8 = ____	56 ÷ 8 = ____
48 ÷ 8 = ____	24 ÷ 8 = ____	72 ÷ 8 = ____	8 ÷ 8 = ____	32 ÷ 8 = ____
24 ÷ 8 = ____	56 ÷ 8 = ____	16 ÷ 8 = ____	40 ÷ 8 = ____	64 ÷ 8 = ____
56 ÷ 8 = ____	32 ÷ 8 = ____	48 ÷ 8 = ____	72 ÷ 8 = ____	8 ÷ 8 = ____
32 ÷ 8 = ____	64 ÷ 8 = ____	24 ÷ 8 = ____	16 ÷ 8 = ____	40 ÷ 8 = ____
64 ÷ 8 = ____	8 ÷ 8 = ____	56 ÷ 8 = ____	48 ÷ 8 = ____	72 ÷ 8 = ____
8 ÷ 8 = ____	40 ÷ 8 = ____	32 ÷ 8 = ____	24 ÷ 8 = ____	16 ÷ 8 = ____
40 ÷ 8 = ____	72 ÷ 8 = ____	64 ÷ 8 = ____	56 ÷ 8 = ____	48 ÷ 8 = ____
72 ÷ 8 = ____	16 ÷ 8 = ____	8 ÷ 8 = ____	32 ÷ 8 = ____	24 ÷ 8 = ____
16 ÷ 8 = ____	48 ÷ 8 = ____	40 ÷ 8 = ____	64 ÷ 8 = ____	56 ÷ 8 = ____
48 ÷ 8 = ____	24 ÷ 8 = ____	72 ÷ 8 = ____	8 ÷ 8 = ____	32 ÷ 8 = ____
24 ÷ 8 = ____	56 ÷ 8 = ____	16 ÷ 8 = ____	40 ÷ 8 = ____	64 ÷ 8 = ____
56 ÷ 8 = ____	32 ÷ 8 = ____	48 ÷ 8 = ____	72 ÷ 8 = ____	8 ÷ 8 = ____
32 ÷ 8 = ____	64 ÷ 8 = ____	24 ÷ 8 = ____	16 ÷ 8 = ____	40 ÷ 8 = ____
64 ÷ 8 = ____	8 ÷ 8 = ____	56 ÷ 8 = ____	48 ÷ 8 = ____	72 ÷ 8 = ____
8 ÷ 8 = ____	40 ÷ 8 = ____	32 ÷ 8 = ____	24 ÷ 8 = ____	16 ÷ 8 = ____
40 ÷ 8 = ____	72 ÷ 8 = ____	64 ÷ 8 = ____	56 ÷ 8 = ____	48 ÷ 8 = ____
72 ÷ 8 = ____	16 ÷ 8 = ____	8 ÷ 8 = ____	32 ÷ 8 = ____	24 ÷ 8 = ____
16 ÷ 8 = ____	48 ÷ 8 = ____	40 ÷ 8 = ____	64 ÷ 8 = ____	56 ÷ 8 = ____
48 ÷ 8 = ____	24 ÷ 8 = ____	72 ÷ 8 = ____	8 ÷ 8 = ____	32 ÷ 8 = ____
24 ÷ 8 = ____	56 ÷ 8 = ____	16 ÷ 8 = ____	40 ÷ 8 = ____	64 ÷ 8 = ____
56 ÷ 8 = ____	32 ÷ 8 = ____	48 ÷ 8 = ____	72 ÷ 8 = ____	8 ÷ 8 = ____
Score: ____/25 ____ Min. ____ Sec.	Score: ____/25 ____ Min. ____ Sec.	Score: ____/25 ____ Min. ____ Sec.	Score: ____/25 ____ Min. ____ Sec.	Score: ____/25 ____ Min. ____ Sec.

Extra Practice Dividing by Eight Drills

Name: _____

Day 1	Day 2	Day 3	Day 4	Day 5
8 ÷ ___ = 1	48 ÷ ___ = 6	___ ÷ 8 = 1	64 ÷ 8 = ___	16 ÷ 8 = ___
___ ÷ 8 = 4	___ ÷ 8 = 9	___ ÷ 8 = 4	24 ÷ 8 = ___	40 ÷ 8 = ___
56 ÷ 8 = ___	8 ÷ 8 = ___	___ ÷ 8 = 7	48 ÷ 8 = ___	64 ÷ 8 = ___
16 ÷ ___ = 2	32 ÷ ___ = 4	___ ÷ 8 = 2	72 ÷ 8 = ___	___ ÷ 8 = 3
___ ÷ 8 = 5	___ ÷ 8 = 7	___ ÷ 8 = 5	8 ÷ 8 = ___	___ ÷ 8 = 6
64 ÷ 8 = ___	16 ÷ 8 = ___	___ ÷ 8 = 8	32 ÷ 8 = ___	___ ÷ 8 = 9
24 ÷ ___ = 3	40 ÷ ___ = 5	___ ÷ 8 = 3	56 ÷ 8 = ___	___ ÷ 8 = 1
___ ÷ 8 = 6	___ ÷ 8 = 8	___ ÷ 8 = 8	16 ÷ 8 = ___	___ ÷ 8 = 4
72 ÷ 8 = ___	24 ÷ 8 = ___	___ ÷ 8 = 9	40 ÷ 8 = ___	___ ÷ 8 = 7
8 ÷ ___ = 1	48 ÷ ___ = 6	___ ÷ 8 = 1	64 ÷ 8 = ___	16 ÷ 8 = ___
32 ÷ ___ = 4	___ ÷ 8 = 9	___ ÷ 8 = 3	24 ÷ 8 = ___	40 ÷ 8 = ___
___ ÷ 8 = 7	8 ÷ 8 = ___	___ ÷ 8 = 7	48 ÷ 8 = ___	64 ÷ 8 = ___
16 ÷ 8 = ___	32 ÷ ___ = 4	___ ÷ 8 = 2	72 ÷ 8 = ___	___ ÷ 8 = 3
40 ÷ 8 = ___	___ ÷ 8 = 7	___ ÷ 8 = 5	8 ÷ 8 = ___	___ ÷ 8 = 6
___ ÷ 8 = 8	16 ÷ 8 = ___	___ ÷ 8 = 8	32 ÷ 8 = ___	___ ÷ 8 = 9
24 ÷ 8 = ___	40 ÷ ___ = 5	___ ÷ 8 = 3	56 ÷ 8 = ___	___ ÷ 8 = 1
48 ÷ ___ = 6	___ ÷ 8 = 8	___ ÷ 8 = 6	16 ÷ 8 = ___	___ ÷ 8 = 4
___ ÷ 8 = 9	24 ÷ 8 = ___	___ ÷ 8 = 9	40 ÷ 8 = ___	___ ÷ 8 = 7
8 ÷ 8 = ___	48 ÷ ___ = 6	___ ÷ 8 = 1	64 ÷ 8 = ___	16 ÷ 8 = ___
32 ÷ ___ = 4	___ ÷ 8 = 9	___ ÷ 8 = 4	24 ÷ 8 = ___	40 ÷ 8 = ___
___ ÷ 8 = 7	8 ÷ 8 = ___	___ ÷ 8 = 7	48 ÷ 8 = ___	64 ÷ 8 = ___
16 ÷ 8 = ___	32 ÷ ___ = 4	___ ÷ 8 = 2	72 ÷ 8 = ___	___ ÷ 8 = 3
40 ÷ ___ = 5	___ ÷ 8 = 7	___ ÷ 8 = 5	8 ÷ 8 = ___	___ ÷ 8 = 6
___ ÷ 8 = 8	16 ÷ 8 = ___	___ ÷ 8 = 8	32 ÷ 8 = ___	___ ÷ 8 = 9
24 ÷ 8 = ___	40 ÷ ___ = 5	___ ÷ 8 = 3	56 ÷ 8 = ___	___ ÷ 8 = 1
Score: ___/25	Score: ___/25	Score: ___/25	Score: ___/25	Score: ___/25
___ Min.	___ Min.	___ Min.	___ Min.	___ Min.
___ Sec.	___ Sec.	___ Sec.	___ Sec.	___ Sec.

OTM-1142 • SSK1-42 Timed Division Facts

Dividing by Eight Review Test

Name: _____

A									
8)8	8)32	8)56	8)16	8)40	8)64	8)24	8)48	8)72	8)8

B									
8)32	8)56	8)16	8)40	8)64	8)24	8)48	8)72	8)8	8)32

C									
8)56	8)32	8)8	8)72	8)24	8)48	8)64	8)40	8)16	8)56

D									
8)16	8)40	8)64	8)24	8)48	8)72	8)8	8)32	8)56	8)16

E									
8)40	8)64	8)24	8)48	8)72	8)8	8)56	8)8	8)16	8)32

F									
8)56	8)16	8)40	8)64	8)24	8)48	8)72	8)32	8)56	8)8

G									
8)16	8)56	8)32	8)48	8)8	8)72	8)24	8)64	8)40	8)16

H									
8)40	8)64	8)24	8)72	8)48	8)8	8)32	8)56	8)16	8)40

I									
8)64	8)48	8)72	8)8	8)24	8)32	8)16	8)40	8)64	8)56

J									
8)24	8)72	8)8	8)40	8)48	8)64	8)32	8)8	8)16	8)48

Date: _____   Score: _____/100   Time: _____ Min. _____ Sec.

Dividing by Nine Drills

Name: _____

Date: Monday _____ Score: _____ /25 Time: _____ Min. _____ Sec.

9 ÷ 9 = ____	27 ÷ 9 = ____	45 ÷ 9 = ____	63 ÷ 9 = ____	81 ÷ 9 = ____
45 ÷ 9 = ____	63 ÷ 9 = ____	81 ÷ 9 = ____	18 ÷ 9 = ____	36 ÷ 9 = ____
81 ÷ 9 = ____	18 ÷ 9 = ____	36 ÷ 9 = ____	72 ÷ 9 = ____	54 ÷ 9 = ____
36 ÷ 9 = ____	72 ÷ 9 = ____	54 ÷ 9 = ____	9 ÷ 9 = ____	27 ÷ 9 = ____
54 ÷ 9 = ____	9 ÷ 9 = ____	27 ÷ 9 = ____	45 ÷ 9 = ____	63 ÷ 9 = ____

Date: Tuesday _____ Score: _____ /25 Time: _____ Min. _____ Sec.

18 ÷ 9 = ____	36 ÷ 9 = ____	72 ÷ 9 = ____	54 ÷ 9 = ____	9 ÷ 9 = ____
72 ÷ 9 = ____	54 ÷ 9 = ____	9 ÷ 9 = ____	27 ÷ 9 = ____	45 ÷ 9 = ____
9 ÷ 9 = ____	27 ÷ 9 = ____	45 ÷ 9 = ____	63 ÷ 9 = ____	81 ÷ 9 = ____
45 ÷ 9 = ____	63 ÷ 9 = ____	81 ÷ 9 = ____	18 ÷ 9 = ____	36 ÷ 9 = ____
81 ÷ 9 = ____	18 ÷ 9 = ____	36 ÷ 9 = ____	72 ÷ 9 = ____	54 ÷ 9 = ____

Date: Wednesday _____ Score: _____ /25 Time: _____ Min. _____ Sec.

27 ÷ 9 = ____	45 ÷ 9 = ____	63 ÷ 9 = ____	81 ÷ 9 = ____	18 ÷ 9 = ____
63 ÷ 9 = ____	81 ÷ 9 = ____	18 ÷ 9 = ____	36 ÷ 9 = ____	72 ÷ 9 = ____
18 ÷ 9 = ____	36 ÷ 9 = ____	72 ÷ 9 = ____	54 ÷ 9 = ____	9 ÷ 9 = ____
72 ÷ 9 = ____	54 ÷ 9 = ____	9 ÷ 9 = ____	27 ÷ 9 = ____	45 ÷ 9 = ____
9 ÷ 9 = ____	27 ÷ 9 = ____	45 ÷ 9 = ____	63 ÷ 9 = ____	81 ÷ 9 = ____

Date: Thursday _____ Score: _____ /25 Time: _____ Min. _____ Sec.

36 ÷ 9 = ____	72 ÷ 9 = ____	54 ÷ 9 = ____	9 ÷ 9 = ____	27 ÷ 9 = ____
54 ÷ 9 = ____	9 ÷ 9 = ____	27 ÷ 9 = ____	45 ÷ 9 = ____	63 ÷ 9 = ____
27 ÷ 9 = ____	45 ÷ 9 = ____	63 ÷ 9 = ____	81 ÷ 9 = ____	18 ÷ 9 = ____
63 ÷ 9 = ____	81 ÷ 9 = ____	18 ÷ 9 = ____	36 ÷ 9 = ____	72 ÷ 9 = ____
18 ÷ 9 = ____	36 ÷ 9 = ____	72 ÷ 9 = ____	54 ÷ 9 = ____	9 ÷ 9 = ____

Date: Friday _____ Score: _____ /25 Time: _____ Min. _____ Sec.

45 ÷ 9 = ____	63 ÷ 9 = ____	81 ÷ 9 = ____	18 ÷ 9 = ____	36 ÷ 9 = ____
81 ÷ 9 = ____	18 ÷ 9 = ____	36 ÷ 9 = ____	72 ÷ 9 = ____	54 ÷ 9 = ____
36 ÷ 9 = ____	72 ÷ 9 = ____	54 ÷ 9 = ____	9 ÷ 9 = ____	27 ÷ 9 = ____
54 ÷ 9 = ____	9 ÷ 9 = ____	27 ÷ 9 = ____	45 ÷ 9 = ____	63 ÷ 9 = ____
27 ÷ 9 = ____	45 ÷ 9 = ____	63 ÷ 9 = ____	81 ÷ 9 = ____	18 ÷ 9 = ____

Home Practice Dividing by Nine Drills

Name: _____

Monday	Tuesday	Wednesday	Thursday	Friday
27 ÷ 9 = _____	9 ÷ 9 = _____	18 ÷ 9 = _____	36 ÷ 9 = _____	45 ÷ 9 = _____
63 ÷ 9 = _____	45 ÷ 9 = _____	72 ÷ 9 = _____	54 ÷ 9 = _____	81 ÷ 9 = _____
18 ÷ 9 = _____	81 ÷ 9 = _____	9 ÷ 9 = _____	27 ÷ 9 = _____	36 ÷ 9 = _____
72 ÷ 9 = _____	36 ÷ 9 = _____	36 ÷ 9 = _____	45 ÷ 9 = _____	54 ÷ 9 = _____
9 ÷ 9 = _____	54 ÷ 9 = _____	81 ÷ 9 = _____	18 ÷ 9 = _____	27 ÷ 9 = _____
45 ÷ 9 = _____	27 ÷ 9 = _____	36 ÷ 9 = _____	72 ÷ 9 = _____	63 ÷ 9 = _____
81 ÷ 9 = _____	63 ÷ 9 = _____	54 ÷ 9 = _____	9 ÷ 9 = _____	18 ÷ 9 = _____
36 ÷ 9 = _____	18 ÷ 9 = _____	27 ÷ 9 = _____	45 ÷ 9 = _____	72 ÷ 9 = _____
54 ÷ 9 = _____	72 ÷ 9 = _____	63 ÷ 9 = _____	81 ÷ 9 = _____	9 ÷ 9 = _____
27 ÷ 9 = _____	9 ÷ 9 = _____	18 ÷ 9 = _____	36 ÷ 9 = _____	45 ÷ 9 = _____
63 ÷ 9 = _____	45 ÷ 9 = _____	72 ÷ 9 = _____	54 ÷ 9 = _____	81 ÷ 9 = _____
18 ÷ 9 = _____	81 ÷ 9 = _____	9 ÷ 9 = _____	27 ÷ 9 = _____	36 ÷ 9 = _____
72 ÷ 9 = _____	36 ÷ 9 = _____	45 ÷ 9 = _____	63 ÷ 9 = _____	54 ÷ 9 = _____
9 ÷ 9 = _____	54 ÷ 9 = _____	81 ÷ 9 = _____	18 ÷ 9 = _____	27 ÷ 9 = _____
45 ÷ 9 = _____	27 ÷ 9 = _____	36 ÷ 9 = _____	72 ÷ 9 = _____	63 ÷ 9 = _____
81 ÷ 9 = _____	63 ÷ 9 = _____	54 ÷ 9 = _____	9 ÷ 9 = _____	18 ÷ 9 = _____
36 ÷ 9 = _____	18 ÷ 9 = _____	27 ÷ 9 = _____	45 ÷ 9 = _____	72 ÷ 9 = _____
54 ÷ 9 = _____	72 ÷ 9 = _____	63 ÷ 9 = _____	81 ÷ 9 = _____	9 ÷ 9 = _____
27 ÷ 9 = _____	9 ÷ 9 = _____	18 ÷ 9 = _____	36 ÷ 9 = _____	45 ÷ 9 = _____
63 ÷ 9 = _____	45 ÷ 9 = _____	72 ÷ 9 = _____	54 ÷ 9 = _____	81 ÷ 9 = _____
18 ÷ 9 = _____	81 ÷ 9 = _____	9 ÷ 9 = _____	27 ÷ 9 = _____	36 ÷ 9 = _____
72 ÷ 9 = _____	36 ÷ 9 = _____	45 ÷ 9 = _____	63 ÷ 9 = _____	54 ÷ 9 = _____
9 ÷ 9 = _____	54 ÷ 9 = _____	81 ÷ 9 = _____	18 ÷ 9 = _____	27 ÷ 9 = _____
45 ÷ 9 = _____	27 ÷ 9 = _____	36 ÷ 9 = _____	72 ÷ 9 = _____	63 ÷ 9 = _____
81 ÷ 9 = _____	63 ÷ 9 = _____	54 ÷ 9 = _____	9 ÷ 9 = _____	18 ÷ 9 = _____
Score: _____ /25	Score: _____ /25	Score: _____ /25	Score: _____ /25	Score: _____ /25
_____ Min. _____ Sec.	_____ Min. _____ Sec.	_____ Min. _____ Sec.	_____ Min. _____ Sec.	_____ Min. _____ Sec.

Day 1	Day 2	Day 3	Day 4	Day 5
$9 \div \_\_\_ = 1$	$54 \div \_\_\_ = 6$	$\_\_\_ \div 9 = 8$	$18 \div 9 = \_\_\_$	$72 \div 9 = \_\_\_$
$\_\_\_ \div 9 = 4$	$\_\_\_ \div 9 = 9$	$\_\_\_ \div 9 = 3$	$45 \div 9 = \_\_\_$	$27 \div 9 = \_\_\_$
$63 \div 9 = \_\_\_$	$9 \div 9 = \_\_\_$	$\_\_\_ \div 9 = 6$	$72 \div 9 = \_\_\_$	$54 \div 9 = \_\_\_$
$18 \div \_\_\_ = 2$	$36 \div \_\_\_ = 4$	$\_\_\_ \div 9 = 9$	$27 \div 9 = \_\_\_$	$\_\_\_ \div 9 = 9$
$\_\_\_ \div 9 = 5$	$\_\_\_ \div 9 = 7$	$\_\_\_ \div 9 = 1$	$54 \div 9 = \_\_\_$	$\_\_\_ \div 9 = 1$
$72 \div 9 = \_\_\_$	$18 \div 9 = \_\_\_$	$\_\_\_ \div 9 = 4$	$81 \div 9 = \_\_\_$	$\_\_\_ \div 9 = 4$
$27 \div \_\_\_ = 3$	$45 \div \_\_\_ = 5$	$\_\_\_ \div 9 = 7$	$9 \div 9 = \_\_\_$	$\_\_\_ \div 9 = 7$
$\_\_\_ \div 9 = 6$	$\_\_\_ \div 9 = 8$	$\_\_\_ \div 9 = 2$	$36 \div 9 = \_\_\_$	$\_\_\_ \div 9 = 2$
$81 \div 9 = \_\_\_$	$27 \div 9 = \_\_\_$	$\_\_\_ \div 9 = 5$	$63 \div 9 = \_\_\_$	$\_\_\_ \div 9 = 5$
$63 \div \_\_\_ = 7$	$54 \div \_\_\_ = 6$	$\_\_\_ \div 9 = 8$	$18 \div 9 = \_\_\_$	$9 \div 9 = \_\_\_$
$\_\_\_ \div 9 = 1$	$\_\_\_ \div 9 = 9$	$\_\_\_ \div 9 = 3$	$45 \div 9 = \_\_\_$	$36 \div 9 = \_\_\_$
$36 \div 9 = \_\_\_$	$9 \div 9 = \_\_\_$	$\_\_\_ \div 9 = 6$	$72 \div 9 = \_\_\_$	$63 \div 9 = \_\_\_$
$18 \div \_\_\_ = 2$	$63 \div \_\_\_ = 7$	$\_\_\_ \div 9 = 9$	$27 \div 9 = \_\_\_$	$\_\_\_ \div 9 = 8$
$\_\_\_ \div 9 = 5$	$\_\_\_ \div 9 = 2$	$\_\_\_ \div 9 = 1$	$54 \div 9 = \_\_\_$	$\_\_\_ \div 9 = 3$
$72 \div 9 = \_\_\_$	$36 \div 9 = \_\_\_$	$\_\_\_ \div 9 = 4$	$81 \div 9 = \_\_\_$	$\_\_\_ \div 9 = 6$
$27 \div \_\_\_ = 3$	$45 \div \_\_\_ = 5$	$\_\_\_ \div 9 = 7$	$9 \div 9 = \_\_\_$	$\_\_\_ \div 9 = 9$
$\_\_\_ \div 9 = 6$	$\_\_\_ \div 9 = 8$	$\_\_\_ \div 9 = 2$	$36 \div 9 = \_\_\_$	$\_\_\_ \div 9 = 2$
$81 \div 9 = \_\_\_$	$27 \div 9 = \_\_\_$	$\_\_\_ \div 9 = 5$	$63 \div 9 = \_\_\_$	$\_\_\_ \div 9 = 5$
$36 \div \_\_\_ = 4$	$54 \div \_\_\_ = 6$	$\_\_\_ \div 9 = 8$	$18 \div 9 = \_\_\_$	$27 \div 9 = \_\_\_$
$9 \div 9 = \_\_\_$	$\_\_\_ \div 9 = 9$	$\_\_\_ \div 9 = 3$	$45 \div 9 = \_\_\_$	$18 \div 9 = \_\_\_$
$63 \div \_\_\_ = 7$	$45 \div 9 = \_\_\_$	$\_\_\_ \div 9 = 6$	$72 \div 9 = \_\_\_$	$45 \div 9 = \_\_\_$
$\_\_\_ \div 9 = 2$	$9 \div \_\_\_ = 1$	$\_\_\_ \div 9 = 9$	$27 \div 9 = \_\_\_$	$\_\_\_ \div 9 = 6$
$45 \div 9 = \_\_\_$	$\_\_\_ \div 9 = 6$	$\_\_\_ \div 9 = 1$	$54 \div 9 = \_\_\_$	$\_\_\_ \div 9 = 9$
$72 \div \_\_\_ = 8$	$63 \div 9 = \_\_\_$	$\_\_\_ \div 9 = 4$	$81 \div 9 = \_\_\_$	$\_\_\_ \div 9 = 1$
$\_\_\_ \div 9 = 3$	$18 \div \_\_\_ = 9$	$\_\_\_ \div 9 = 7$	$9 \div 9 = \_\_\_$	$\_\_\_ \div 9 = 4$
Score: _____/25	Score: _____/25	Score: _____/25	Score: _____/25	Score: _____/25
_____ Min.	_____ Min.	_____ Min.	_____ Min.	_____ Min.
_____ Sec.	_____ Sec.	_____ Sec.	_____ Sec.	_____ Sec.

Dividing by Nine Review Test

Name: _____

A									
$9\overline{)\,9}$	$9\overline{)\,36}$	$9\overline{)\,63}$	$9\overline{)\,18}$	$9\overline{)\,45}$	$9\overline{)\,72}$	$9\overline{)\,27}$	$9\overline{)\,54}$	$9\overline{)\,81}$	$9\overline{)\,9}$

B									
$9\overline{)\,63}$	$9\overline{)\,27}$	$9\overline{)\,54}$	$9\overline{)\,36}$	$9\overline{)\,81}$	$9\overline{)\,9}$	$9\overline{)\,36}$	$9\overline{)\,63}$	$9\overline{)\,18}$	$9\overline{)\,45}$

C									
$9\overline{)\,18}$	$9\overline{)\,72}$	$9\overline{)\,27}$	$9\overline{)\,54}$	$9\overline{)\,9}$	$9\overline{)\,36}$	$9\overline{)\,81}$	$9\overline{)\,18}$	$9\overline{)\,72}$	$9\overline{)\,63}$

D									
$9\overline{)\,45}$	$9\overline{)\,18}$	$9\overline{)\,63}$	$9\overline{)\,81}$	$9\overline{)\,45}$	$9\overline{)\,9}$	$9\overline{)\,36}$	$9\overline{)\,54}$	$9\overline{)\,45}$	$9\overline{)\,27}$

E									
$9\overline{)\,72}$	$9\overline{)\,27}$	$9\overline{)\,72}$	$9\overline{)\,54}$	$9\overline{)\,81}$	$9\overline{)\,63}$	$9\overline{)\,18}$	$9\overline{)\,9}$	$9\overline{)\,45}$	$9\overline{)\,36}$

F									
$9\overline{)\,54}$	$9\overline{)\,81}$	$9\overline{)\,9}$	$9\overline{)\,72}$	$9\overline{)\,36}$	$9\overline{)\,45}$	$9\overline{)\,72}$	$9\overline{)\,27}$	$9\overline{)\,63}$	$9\overline{)\,18}$

G									
$9\overline{)\,9}$	$9\overline{)\,27}$	$9\overline{)\,54}$	$9\overline{)\,36}$	$9\overline{)\,63}$	$9\overline{)\,81}$	$9\overline{)\,18}$	$9\overline{)\,45}$	$9\overline{)\,72}$	$9\overline{)\,27}$

H									
$9\overline{)\,54}$	$9\overline{)\,81}$	$9\overline{)\,9}$	$9\overline{)\,36}$	$9\overline{)\,18}$	$9\overline{)\,63}$	$9\overline{)\,45}$	$9\overline{)\,72}$	$9\overline{)\,27}$	$9\overline{)\,54}$

I									
$9\overline{)\,9}$	$9\overline{)\,36}$	$9\overline{)\,18}$	$9\overline{)\,81}$	$9\overline{)\,63}$	$9\overline{)\,45}$	$9\overline{)\,72}$	$9\overline{)\,27}$	$9\overline{)\,54}$	$9\overline{)\,81}$

J									
$9\overline{)\,36}$	$9\overline{)\,63}$	$9\overline{)\,9}$	$9\overline{)\,18}$	$9\overline{)\,45}$	$9\overline{)\,72}$	$9\overline{)\,27}$	$9\overline{)\,54}$	$9\overline{)\,81}$	$9\overline{)\,9}$

Date: _____   Score: _____/100   Time: _____ Min. _____ Sec.

 OTM-1142 • SSK1-42 Timed Division Facts

Row 1	Row 2	Row 3	Row 4
40 ÷ 8 = _____	6 ÷ 6 = _____	48 ÷ 8 = _____	42 ÷ 7 = _____
32 ÷ 8 = _____	36 ÷ 6 = _____	81 ÷ 9 = _____	35 ÷ 7 = _____
72 ÷ 9 = _____	28 ÷ 7 = _____	24 ÷ 6 = _____	48 ÷ 8 = _____
28 ÷ 7 = _____	27 ÷ 9 = _____	63 ÷ 9 = _____	12 ÷ 6 = _____
49 ÷ 7 = _____	72 ÷ 9 = _____	24 ÷ 8 = _____	48 ÷ 6 = _____
81 ÷ 9 = _____	35 ÷ 7 = _____	30 ÷ 6 = _____	32 ÷ 8 = _____
6 ÷ 6 = _____	24 ÷ 8 = _____	42 ÷ 7 = _____	45 ÷ 9 = _____
27 ÷ 9 = _____	49 ÷ 7 = _____	48 ÷ 6 = _____	42 ÷ 7 = _____
72 ÷ 8 = _____	18 ÷ 9 = _____	40 ÷ 8 = _____	6 ÷ 6 = _____
42 ÷ 6 = _____	64 ÷ 8 = _____	21 ÷ 7 = _____	18 ÷ 9 = _____
36 ÷ 9 = _____	21 ÷ 7 = _____	36 ÷ 6 = _____	36 ÷ 6 = _____
30 ÷ 6 = _____	32 ÷ 8 = _____	49 ÷ 7 = _____	54 ÷ 9 = _____
24 ÷ 8 = _____	48 ÷ 6 = _____	56 ÷ 8 = _____	49 ÷ 7 = _____
72 ÷ 8 = _____	30 ÷ 6 = _____	27 ÷ 9 = _____	8 ÷ 8 = _____
21 ÷ 7 = _____	63 ÷ 9 = _____	16 ÷ 8 = _____	42 ÷ 6 = _____
56 ÷ 7 = _____	36 ÷ 9 = _____	45 ÷ 9 = _____	18 ÷ 6 = _____
18 ÷ 6 = _____	40 ÷ 8 = _____	56 ÷ 7 = _____	63 ÷ 9 = _____
63 ÷ 7 = _____	24 ÷ 6 = _____	18 ÷ 9 = _____	64 ÷ 8 = _____
48 ÷ 8 = _____	12 ÷ 6 = _____	72 ÷ 9 = _____	28 ÷ 7 = _____
36 ÷ 6 = _____	16 ÷ 8 = _____	35 ÷ 7 = _____	18 ÷ 9 = _____
8 ÷ 8 = _____	54 ÷ 6 = _____	54 ÷ 9 = _____	14 ÷ 7 = _____
54 ÷ 9 = _____	14 ÷ 7 = _____	12 ÷ 6 = _____	49 ÷ 7 = _____
56 ÷ 8 = _____	56 ÷ 8 = _____	14 ÷ 7 = _____	81 ÷ 9 = _____
9 ÷ 9 = _____	56 ÷ 7 = _____	54 ÷ 6 = _____	54 ÷ 6 = _____
63 ÷ 7 = _____	45 ÷ 9 = _____	64 ÷ 8 = _____	24 ÷ 6 = _____

Date: _____ Score: _____/100 Time: _____ Min. _____ Sec.

Timed Drill Review for Dividing by 6, 7, 8, and 9

Name: _____

A $8\overline{)40}$	$8\overline{)32}$	$9\overline{)72}$	$7\overline{)28}$	$7\overline{)49}$	$9\overline{)81}$	$6\overline{)6}$	$9\overline{)27}$	$8\overline{)72}$	$6\overline{)42}$
B $9\overline{)36}$	$6\overline{)30}$	$8\overline{)24}$	$8\overline{)72}$	$7\overline{)21}$	$7\overline{)56}$	$6\overline{)18}$	$7\overline{)63}$	$8\overline{)48}$	$6\overline{)36}$
C $8\overline{)8}$	$9\overline{)54}$	$8\overline{)56}$	$9\overline{)9}$	$7\overline{)63}$	$6\overline{)6}$	$6\overline{)36}$	$7\overline{)28}$	$9\overline{)27}$	$9\overline{)72}$
D $7\overline{)35}$	$8\overline{)24}$	$7\overline{)49}$	$9\overline{)18}$	$8\overline{)64}$	$7\overline{)21}$	$8\overline{)32}$	$6\overline{)48}$	$6\overline{)30}$	$9\overline{)63}$
E $9\overline{)36}$	$8\overline{)40}$	$6\overline{)24}$	$6\overline{)12}$	$8\overline{)16}$	$6\overline{)54}$	$7\overline{)14}$	$8\overline{)56}$	$7\overline{)56}$	$9\overline{)45}$
F $8\overline{)48}$	$9\overline{)81}$	$6\overline{)24}$	$9\overline{)63}$	$8\overline{)24}$	$6\overline{)30}$	$7\overline{)42}$	$6\overline{)48}$	$8\overline{)40}$	$7\overline{)21}$
G $6\overline{)36}$	$7\overline{)49}$	$8\overline{)56}$	$9\overline{)27}$	$8\overline{)16}$	$9\overline{)45}$	$7\overline{)56}$	$9\overline{)18}$	$9\overline{)72}$	$7\overline{)35}$
H $9\overline{)54}$	$6\overline{)12}$	$7\overline{)14}$	$6\overline{)54}$	$8\overline{)64}$	$7\overline{)42}$	$7\overline{)35}$	$8\overline{)48}$	$6\overline{)12}$	$6\overline{)48}$
I $8\overline{)32}$	$9\overline{)45}$	$7\overline{)42}$	$6\overline{)6}$	$9\overline{)18}$	$8\overline{)16}$	$9\overline{)54}$	$7\overline{)49}$	$8\overline{)8}$	$6\overline{)42}$
J $6\overline{)18}$	$9\overline{)63}$	$8\overline{)64}$	$7\overline{)28}$	$9\overline{)18}$	$7\overline{)14}$	$7\overline{)49}$	$9\overline{)81}$	$6\overline{)54}$	$6\overline{)24}$

Date: _____ Score: _____ /100 Time: _____ Min. _____ Sec.

Timed Drill Review Using Divisors 2 to 9

Name: _____

Row 1	Row 2	Row 3	Row 4
$30 \div 5 =$ _____	$40 \div 8 =$ _____	$24 \div 3 =$ _____	$6 \div 6 =$ _____
$12 \div 2 =$ _____	$32 \div 8 =$ _____	$28 \div 4 =$ _____	$36 \div 6 =$ _____
$27 \div 3 =$ _____	$72 \div 9 =$ _____	$40 \div 5 =$ _____	$28 \div 7 =$ _____
$12 \div 4 =$ _____	$28 \div 7 =$ _____	$10 \div 2 =$ _____	$27 \div 9 =$ _____
$10 \div 5 =$ _____	$49 \div 7 =$ _____	$12 \div 3 =$ _____	$72 \div 9 =$ _____
$18 \div 2 =$ _____	$81 \div 9 =$ _____	$20 \div 4 =$ _____	$35 \div 7 =$ _____
$6 \div 3 =$ _____	$6 \div 6 =$ _____	$15 \div 5 =$ _____	$24 \div 8 =$ _____
$24 \div 4 =$ _____	$27 \div 9 =$ _____	$16 \div 2 =$ _____	$49 \div 7 =$ _____
$35 \div 5 =$ _____	$72 \div 8 =$ _____	$3 \div 3 =$ _____	$18 \div 9 =$ _____
$4 \div 2 =$ _____	$42 \div 6 =$ _____	$4 \div 4 =$ _____	$64 \div 8 =$ _____
$21 \div 3 =$ _____	$36 \div 9 =$ _____	$5 \div 5 =$ _____	$21 \div 7 =$ _____
$16 \div 4 =$ _____	$63 \div 9 =$ _____	$6 \div 2 =$ _____	$32 \div 8 =$ _____
$20 \div 5 =$ _____	$24 \div 8 =$ _____	$18 \div 3 =$ _____	$48 \div 6 =$ _____
$2 \div 2 =$ _____	$72 \div 8 =$ _____	$32 \div 4 =$ _____	$30 \div 6 =$ _____
$9 \div 3 =$ _____	$42 \div 7 =$ _____	$30 \div 5 =$ _____	$63 \div 9 =$ _____
$8 \div 4 =$ _____	$56 \div 7 =$ _____	$12 \div 2 =$ _____	$36 \div 9 =$ _____
$45 \div 5 =$ _____	$18 \div 6 =$ _____	$27 \div 3 =$ _____	$40 \div 8 =$ _____
$8 \div 2 =$ _____	$7 \div 7 =$ _____	$36 \div 4 =$ _____	$24 \div 6 =$ _____
$15 \div 3 =$ _____	$48 \div 8 =$ _____	$10 \div 5 =$ _____	$12 \div 6 =$ _____
$20 \div 4 =$ _____	$36 \div 6 =$ _____	$18 \div 2 =$ _____	$16 \div 8 =$ _____
$25 \div 5 =$ _____	$8 \div 8 =$ _____	$6 \div 3 =$ _____	$54 \div 6 =$ _____
$14 \div 2 =$ _____	$54 \div 9 =$ _____	$12 \div 4 =$ _____	$14 \div 7 =$ _____
$24 \div 3 =$ _____	$56 \div 8 =$ _____	$35 \div 5 =$ _____	$56 \div 8 =$ _____
$36 \div 4 =$ _____	$9 \div 9 =$ _____	$2 \div 2 =$ _____	$56 \div 7 =$ _____
$40 \div 5 =$ _____	$63 \div 7 =$ _____	$21 \div 3 =$ _____	$45 \div 9 =$ _____

Date: _____ Score: _____/100 Time: _____ Min. _____ Sec.

Timed Drill Review Using Divisors 1 to 9

Name: _____

A									
$9\overline{)63}$	$6\overline{)24}$	$4\overline{)4}$	$9\overline{)18}$	$1\overline{)7}$	$8\overline{)32}$	$5\overline{)15}$	$3\overline{)12}$	$1\overline{)8}$	$2\overline{)16}$

B									
$7\overline{)42}$	$1\overline{)5}$	$3\overline{)24}$	$2\overline{)16}$	$5\overline{)45}$	$8\overline{)64}$	$2\overline{)14}$	$8\overline{)72}$	$4\overline{)8}$	$9\overline{)81}$

C									
$6\overline{)36}$	$3\overline{)27}$	$4\overline{)28}$	$8\overline{)16}$	$1\overline{)9}$	$7\overline{)21}$	$4\overline{)28}$	$5\overline{)10}$	$5\overline{)25}$	$3\overline{)9}$

D									
$7\overline{)7}$	$8\overline{)48}$	$1\overline{)3}$	$6\overline{)30}$	$2\overline{)8}$	$9\overline{)36}$	$4\overline{)20}$	$6\overline{)12}$	$1\overline{)8}$	$7\overline{)49}$

E									
$5\overline{)5}$	$8\overline{)40}$	$2\overline{)8}$	$3\overline{)3}$	$8\overline{)32}$	$6\overline{)54}$	$8\overline{)56}$	$6\overline{)12}$	$2\overline{)10}$	$9\overline{)72}$

F									
$4\overline{)12}$	$5\overline{)35}$	$6\overline{)6}$	$9\overline{)36}$	$3\overline{)21}$	$1\overline{)6}$	$7\overline{)28}$	$2\overline{)4}$	$5\overline{)20}$	$4\overline{)32}$

G									
$6\overline{)18}$	$7\overline{)21}$	$3\overline{)15}$	$7\overline{)63}$	$9\overline{)9}$	$4\overline{)24}$	$7\overline{)14}$	$1\overline{)4}$	$6\overline{)42}$	$9\overline{)27}$

H									
$2\overline{)2}$	$5\overline{)40}$	$8\overline{)24}$	$4\overline{)16}$	$9\overline{)45}$	$1\overline{)1}$	$7\overline{)56}$	$3\overline{)6}$	$8\overline{)8}$	$6\overline{)48}$

I									
$5\overline{)20}$	$2\overline{)12}$	$7\overline{)35}$	$2\overline{)6}$	$9\overline{)54}$	$3\overline{)18}$	$3\overline{)24}$	$5\overline{)30}$	$1\overline{)2}$	$4\overline{)36}$

J									
$8\overline{)64}$	$7\overline{)42}$	$1\overline{)5}$	$3\overline{)24}$	$2\overline{)16}$	$5\overline{)45}$	$8\overline{)64}$	$2\overline{)14}$	$8\overline{)72}$	$4\overline{)24}$

Date: _____ Score: _____/100 Time: _____ Min. _____ Sec.

Timed Drill Review Using Divisors 1 to 9

Name: _____

A									
4)‾20	9)‾36	2)‾8	6)‾30	1)‾3	8)‾48	7)‾7	3)‾9	1)‾8	7)‾49

B									
5)‾5	8)‾40	2)‾18	3)‾3	8)‾32	6)‾54	5)‾10	4)‾28	7)‾21	1)‾9

C									
8)‾16	4)‾28	3)‾27	6)‾36	7)‾42	1)‾5	3)‾24	2)‾16	5)‾45	8)‾64

D									
2)‾14	8)‾72	3)‾21	9)‾36	6)‾6	5)‾35	4)‾12	9)‾72	2)‾10	6)‾12

E									
7)‾28	2)‾4	5)‾20	4)‾32	6)‾18	7)‾21	3)‾15	7)‾63	9)‾9	4)‾24

F									
7)‾14	1)‾4	6)‾42	9)‾27	2)‾2	5)‾40	8)‾24	9)‾45	1)‾1	7)‾56

G									
3)‾6	8)‾8	6)‾48	5)‾20	2)‾12	8)‾64	4)‾36	1)‾2	5)‾30	3)‾24

H									
3)‾18	9)‾54	2)‾6	1)‾8	3)‾12	5)‾15	8)‾32	1)‾7	9)‾18	4)‾4

I									
6)‾24	9)‾63	4)‾8	8)‾72	2)‾14	8)‾64	5)‾45	2)‾16	3)‾24	1)‾5

J									
7)‾42	5)‾10	4)‾28	7)‾21	1)‾9	8)‾16	4)‾28	3)‾27	6)‾36	9)‾81

Date: _____   Score: _____ /100   Time: _____ Min. _____ Sec.

OTM-1142 • SSK1-42 Timed Division Facts

Timed Drill Review Using Divisors 1 to 9

Name: _____

A									
4)8	8)72	2)14	8)64	5)45	2)16	3)24	1)5	7)42	5)10
B									
4)28	7)21	1)9	8)16	4)28	3)27	6)36	9)81	5)25	3)9
C									
7)7	8)48	1)3	6)30	2)8	9)36	4)20	6)54	8)32	3)3
D									
2)18	8)40	5)5	7)49	1)8	6)12	8)56	6)12	2)10	9)72
E									
4)12	5)35	6)6	9)36	3)21	7)63	3)15	7)21	6)18	4)32
F									
5)20	2)4	7)28	1)6	9)9	4)24	7)14	1)4	6)42	9)27
G									
2)2	5)40	8)24	2)12	5)20	6)48	8)8	3)6	7)56	1)1
H									
9)45	4)16	7)35	2)6	9)54	3)18	3)24	5)30	1)2	4)36
I									
8)64	9)63	6)24	4)4	9)18	1)7	8)32	5)15	3)12	1)8
J									
2)16	9)36	3)9	4)12	5)25	6)42	7)49	8)64	9)81	7)35

Date: _____ Score: _____/100 Time: _____ Min. _____ Sec.

© On The Mark Press • S&S Learning Materials   OTM-1142 • SSK1-42 Timed Division Facts

Timed Drill Review Using Divisions 1 to 9

Name: _____

A $36 \div 4 =$ ____	$54 \div 9 =$ ____	$81 \div 3 =$ ____	$40 \div 5 =$ ____	$14 \div 7 =$ ____
B $24 \div 8 =$ ____	$72 \div 9 =$ ____	$48 \div 8 =$ ____	$63 \div 7 =$ ____	$72 \div 8 =$ ____
C $64 \div 8 =$ ____	$4 \div 1 =$ ____	$4 \div 4 =$ ____	$4 \div 2 =$ ____	$63 \div 9 =$ ____
D $25 \div 5 =$ ____	$18 \div 3 =$ ____	$27 \div 9 =$ ____	$54 \div 6 =$ ____	$2 \div 2 =$ ____
E $24 \div 6 =$ ____	$40 \div 5 =$ ____	$24 \div 3 =$ ____	$12 \div 6 =$ ____	$6 \div 1 =$ ____
F $42 \div 6 =$ ____	$16 \div 2 =$ ____	$35 \div 7 =$ ____	$30 \div 6 =$ ____	$12 \div 3 =$ ____
G $81 \div 9 =$ ____	$49 \div 7 =$ ____	$36 \div 9 =$ ____	$6 \div 3 =$ ____	$6 \div 6 =$ ____
H $27 \div 3 =$ ____	$8 \div 8 =$ ____	$9 \div 9 =$ ____	$28 \div 4 =$ ____	$16 \div 4 =$ ____
I $12 \div 2 =$ ____	$36 \div 9 =$ ____	$8 \div 4 =$ ____	$21 \div 7 =$ ____	$1 \div 1 =$ ____
J $30 \div 5 =$ ____	$18 \div 6 =$ ____	$15 \div 5 =$ ____	$18 \div 2 =$ ____	$72 \div 8 =$ ____
K $2 \div 1 =$ ____	$30 \div 6 =$ ____	$5 \div 5 =$ ____	$56 \div 7 =$ ____	$35 \div 5 =$ ____
L $5 \div 1 =$ ____	$7 \div 7 =$ ____	$6 \div 2 =$ ____	$18 \div 9 =$ ____	$7 \div 1 =$ ____
M $32 \div 4 =$ ____	$15 \div 3 =$ ____	$45 \div 5 =$ ____	$48 \div 6 =$ ____	$10 \div 2 =$ ____
N $56 \div 8 =$ ____	$9 \div 3 =$ ____	$3 \div 1 =$ ____	$40 \div 8 =$ ____	$12 \div 4 =$ ____
O $28 \div 7 =$ ____	$14 \div 2 =$ ____	$18 \div 6 =$ ____	$42 \div 7 =$ ____	$20 \div 4 =$ ____
P $24 \div 8 =$ ____	$27 \div 9 =$ ____	$20 \div 5 =$ ____	$21 \div 3 =$ ____	$8 \div 2 =$ ____
Q $35 \div 5 =$ ____	$21 \div 3 =$ ____	$20 \div 4 =$ ____	$27 \div 9 =$ ____	$24 \div 8 =$ ____
R $35 \div 7 =$ ____	$16 \div 8 =$ ____	$45 \div 9 =$ ____	$8 \div 1 =$ ____	$36 \div 4 =$ ____
S $72 \div 9 =$ ____	$63 \div 8 =$ ____	$56 \div 7 =$ ____	$45 \div 9 =$ ____	$42 \div 6 =$ ____
T $27 \div 9 =$ ____	$14 \div 2 =$ ____	$16 \div 8 =$ ____	$20 \div 5 =$ ____	$30 \div 6 =$ ____

Date: _____ Score: _____/100 Time: _____ Min. _____ Sec.

© On The Mark Press • S&S Learning Materials OTM-1142 • SSK1-42 Timed Division Facts

Name: _____

A $35 \div 5 =$ ____	$36 \div 6 =$ ____	$4 \div 2 =$ ____	$64 \div 8 =$ ____	$32 \div 8 =$ ____
B $56 \div 7 =$ ____	$16 \div 2 =$ ____	$18 \div 6 =$ ____	$9 \div 3 =$ ____	$48 \div 6 =$ ____
C $21 \div 3 =$ ____	$9 \div 9 =$ ____	$48 \div 8 =$ ____	$63 \div 7 =$ ____	$27 \div 9 =$ ____
D $10 \div 2 =$ ____	$36 \div 9 =$ ____	$4 \div 1 =$ ____	$24 \div 4 =$ ____	$81 \div 9 =$ ____
E $21 \div 7 =$ ____	$2 \div 2 =$ ____	$54 \div 6 =$ ____	$42 \div 7 =$ ____	$40 \div 5 =$ ____
F $49 \div 7 =$ ____	$6 \div 1 =$ ____	$8 \div 4 =$ ____	$7 \div 1 =$ ____	$32 \div 4 =$ ____
G $3 \div 1 =$ ____	$12 \div 4 =$ ____	$8 \div 1 =$ ____	$12 \div 6 =$ ____	$72 \div 8 =$ ____
H $24 \div 3 =$ ____	$20 \div 5 =$ ____	$16 \div 8 =$ ____	$56 \div 7 =$ ____	$27 \div 9 =$ ____
I $32 \div 4 =$ ____	$63 \div 9 =$ ____	$40 \div 8 =$ ____	$14 \div 2 =$ ____	$6 \div 3 =$ ____
J $14 \div 7 =$ ____	$1 \div 1 =$ ____	$30 \div 6 =$ ____	$12 \div 3 =$ ____	$64 \div 8 =$ ____
K $49 \div 7 =$ ____	$8 \div 8 =$ ____	$42 \div 6 =$ ____	$5 \div 5 =$ ____	$28 \div 4 =$ ____
L $24 \div 8 =$ ____	$8 \div 2 =$ ____	$4 \div 4 =$ ____	$35 \div 7 =$ ____	$45 \div 9 =$ ____
M $12 \div 2 =$ ____	$30 \div 5 =$ ____	$12 \div 4 =$ ____	$18 \div 3 =$ ____	$45 \div 5 =$ ____
N $27 \div 3 =$ ____	$6 \div 6 =$ ____	$32 \div 8 =$ ____	$5 \div 1 =$ ____	$15 \div 5 =$ ____
O $2 \div 1 =$ ____	$3 \div 3 =$ ____	$42 \div 6 =$ ____	$7 \div 1 =$ ____	$18 \div 2 =$ ____
P $56 \div 8 =$ ____	$7 \div 7 =$ ____	$72 \div 9 =$ ____	$20 \div 4 =$ ____	$36 \div 4 =$ ____
Q $36 \div 6 =$ ____	$28 \div 7 =$ ____	$54 \div 9 =$ ____	$28 \div 4 =$ ____	$9 \div 1 =$ ____
R $25 \div 5 =$ ____	$15 \div 3 =$ ____	$18 \div 9 =$ ____	$24 \div 6 =$ ____	$6 \div 2 =$ ____
S $45 \div 9 =$ ____	$72 \div 9 =$ ____	$24 \div 8 =$ ____	$8 \div 2 =$ ____	$9 \div 3 =$ ____
T $10 \div 5 =$ ____	$12 \div 2 =$ ____	$81 \div 9 =$ ____	$56 \div 7 =$ ____	$48 \div 6 =$ ____

Date: _____ Score: _____/100 Time: ____ Min. ____ Sec.

Timed Drill Review Using Divisions 1 to 9

Name: _____

A $32 \div 8 =$ ___	$40 \div 5 =$ ___	$27 \div 9 =$ ___	$24 \div 8 =$ ___	$20 \div 4 =$ ___
B $64 \div 8 =$ ___	$42 \div 7 =$ ___	$32 \div 4 =$ ___	$18 \div 3 =$ ___	$72 \div 9 =$ ___
C $4 \div 2 =$ ___	$6 \div 1 =$ ___	$63 \div 9 =$ ___	$12 \div 4 =$ ___	$25 \div 5 =$ ___
D $36 \div 6 =$ ___	$54 \div 6 =$ ___	$40 \div 8 =$ ___	$30 \div 5 =$ ___	$9 \div 1 =$ ___
E $35 \div 5 =$ ___	$2 \div 2 =$ ___	$14 \div 2 =$ ___	$12 \div 2 =$ ___	$28 \div 4 =$ ___
F $48 \div 6 =$ ___	$21 \div 7 =$ ___	$6 \div 3 =$ ___	$32 \div 8 =$ ___	$54 \div 9 =$ ___
G $9 \div 3 =$ ___	$32 \div 4 =$ ___	$14 \div 7 =$ ___	$6 \div 6 =$ ___	$28 \div 7 =$ ___
H $18 \div 6 =$ ___	$7 \div 1 =$ ___	$1 \div 1 =$ ___	$27 \div 3 =$ ___	$45 \div 5 =$ ___
I $16 \div 2 =$ ___	$8 \div 4 =$ ___	$30 \div 6 =$ ___	$45 \div 5 =$ ___	$6 \div 2 =$ ___
J $56 \div 7 =$ ___	$6 \div 1 =$ ___	$12 \div 3 =$ ___	$42 \div 6 =$ ___	$24 \div 6 =$ ___
K $27 \div 9 =$ ___	$49 \div 7 =$ ___	$64 \div 8 =$ ___	$3 \div 3 =$ ___	$18 \div 9 =$ ___
L $63 \div 7 =$ ___	$72 \div 8 =$ ___	$49 \div 7 =$ ___	$2 \div 1 =$ ___	$15 \div 3 =$ ___
M $48 \div 8 =$ ___	$12 \div 6 =$ ___	$28 \div 4 =$ ___	$15 \div 5 =$ ___	$36 \div 6 =$ ___
N $9 \div 9 =$ ___	$8 \div 1 =$ ___	$5 \div 5 =$ ___	$5 \div 1 =$ ___	$24 \div 8 =$ ___
O $21 \div 3 =$ ___	$12 \div 4 =$ ___	$42 \div 6 =$ ___	$7 \div 7 =$ ___	$20 \div 4 =$ ___
P $81 \div 9 =$ ___	$3 \div 1 =$ ___	$8 \div 8 =$ ___	$56 \div 8 =$ ___	$30 \div 5 =$ ___
Q $24 \div 4 =$ ___	$56 \div 7 =$ ___	$45 \div 9 =$ ___	$18 \div 2 =$ ___	$54 \div 6 =$ ___
R $4 \div 1 =$ ___	$16 \div 8 =$ ___	$35 \div 7 =$ ___	$7 \div 1 =$ ___	$64 \div 8 =$ ___
S $36 \div 9 =$ ___	$20 \div 5 =$ ___	$4 \div 4 =$ ___	$36 \div 6 =$ ___	$32 \div 4 =$ ___
T $10 \div 2 =$ ___	$24 \div 3 =$ ___	$8 \div 2 =$ ___	$36 \div 4 =$ ___	$72 \div 8 =$ ___

Date: _____   Score: _____ /100   Time: _____ Min. _____ Sec.

Score Record Sheet for _____ Drills

Name: _____

1. Date: _____

    Score: ____/25 Time: ____Min. ____Sec.

2. Date: _____

    Score: ____/25 Time: ____Min. ____Sec.

3. Date: _____

    Score: ____/25 Time: ____Min. ____Sec.

4. Date: _____

    Score: ____/25 Time: ____Min. ____Sec.

5. Date: _____

    Score: ____/25 Time: ____Min. ____Sec.

6. Date: _____

    Score: ____/25 Time: ____Min. ____Sec.

7. Date: _____

    Score: ____/25 Time: ____Min. ____Sec.

8. Date: _____

    Score: ____/25 Time: ____Min. ____Sec.

9. Date: _____

    Score: ____/25 Time: ____Min. ____Sec.

10. Date: _____

    Score: ____/25 Time: ____Min. ____Sec.

11. Date: _____

    Score: ____/25 Time: ____Min. ____Sec.

12. Date: _____

    Score: ____/25 Time: ____Min. ____Sec.

My speed and accuracy is

_____ .

Score Record Sheet for _____ Drills

Name: _____

1. Date: _____

    Score: ____/100 Time: ____Min. ____Sec.

2. Date: _____

    Score: ____/100 Time: ____Min. ____Sec.

3. Date: _____

    Score: ____/100 Time: ____Min. ____Sec.

4. Date: _____

    Score: ____/100 Time: ____Min. ____Sec.

5. Date: _____

    Score: ____/100 Time: ____Min. ____Sec.

6. Date: _____

    Score: ____/100 Time: ____Min. ____Sec.

7. Date: _____

    Score: ____/100 Time: ____Min. ____Sec.

8. Date: _____

    Score: ____/100 Time: ____Min. ____Sec.

9. Date: _____

    Score: ____/100 Time: ____Min. ____Sec.

10. Date: _____

    Score: ____/100 Time: ____Min. ____Sec.

11. Date: _____

    Score: ____/100 Time: ____Min. ____Sec.

12. Date: _____

    Score: ____/100 Time: ____Min. ____Sec.

My speed and accuracy is

_____ .

9 781550 359015